INSIGHT POCKE...

W9-BJH-732

MacMillan

Hawaii

Discovery CHANNEL

APA PUBLICATIONS
Part of the Langenscheidt Publishing Group

Hawaiian Islands

50 miles / 30 km

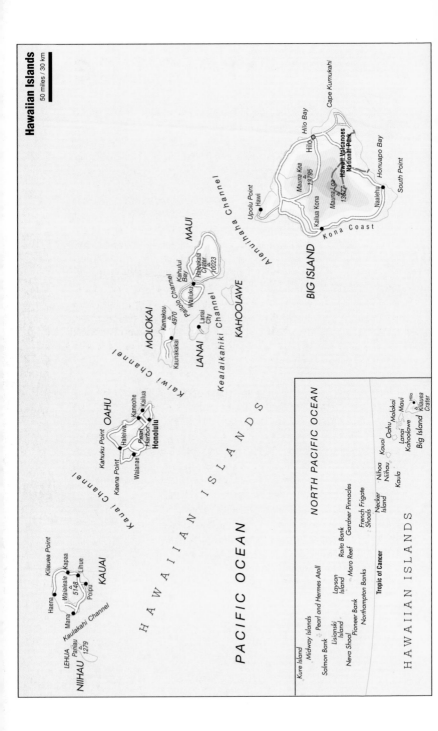

Welcome

This guidebook combines the interests and enthusiasms of two of the world's best-known information providers: Insight Guides, who have set the standard for visual travel guides since 1970, and Discovery Channel, the world's premier source of non-fiction television programming. Its aim is to bring you the best of Hawaii in a series of tailor-made itineraries devised by Insight's Hawaii correspondent, Scott Rutherford.

If ever there was a melting pot of scenery and people, Hawaii is it – from beaches of white or black sands to hidden green valleys and snow-covered mountains, from a spectrum of skin tones to religions and languages of every persuasion. The book begins with a look at the rich history and culture of this incredible 50th state of America. Following this are a series of carefully crafted itineraries – both full- and half-day – covering Oahu, the Big Island, Kauai and Maui. For those who have the luxury of time, there are day trips to the lesser-known, but no less intriguing, islands of Molokai and Lanai. Complementing the itineraries are chapters on shopping, eating out (with a listing of recommended restaurants) nightlife and activities, plus a calendar of special events and a fact-packed practical information section which includes a list of hand-picked hotels.

 Scott Rutherford was first dispatched to Hawaii in 1985 on a book assignment. Unlike most travelers, he by-passed Oahu and went directly to Kauai's north shore, arriving under the turbid shroud of a midnight rain and jet lag. Hours later, a resplendent sunrise evaporated that shroud and the blue-green Hanalei Bay was revealed in all its glory. His seduction was repeated a few evenings later by a woman with a golden smile. The woman, as they've tended to do in Rutherford's nomadic wanderings, left. But Hawaii remained home for several years. Having scoured the most remote corners of the islands several times over, Rutherford is amply qualified to write this book. His suggestions are opinionated at times – sunsets are meant to be worshipped everyday like some cultish liturgy – but always insightful.

Preceding pages: lush, inviting Hawaii coastline
Following pages: winter surfer, Sunset Beach, Oahu

History &Culture

F or such a small and idyllic place in the middle of a beautiful nowhere, Hawaii's history has been an almost non-stop struggle for dominance over land and values. Everyone arriving in Hawaii has always *wanted* something from the islands. The first settlers from the Marquesas wanted refuge. Tahitians wanted what the early Marquesians had, namely, everything. Tribal chiefs fought among themselves for pieces of the islands. A more powerful chief wanted not just one island, but *all* of them. Whalers and missionaries bickered over bodies and souls. Sugar and pineapple barons wanted land and then more land. Twentieth century newcomers wanted – and still do – a parcel of paradise, if not all of it. It's never-ending, this *wanting* of Hawaii. Each new arrival steps on the toes of those who came before, usurping the place of those who feel they are the rightful heirs to the land. But in the beginning, there was nobody.

Natural History

Hawaii is like some student's science project explaining island development and decay, with islands at various evolutionary stages all lined up in chronological order. Hop along the 1,500-mile (2,400-km) long Hawaiian chain and one follows the geological history of the islands, indeed, of any island.

Hawaii sits in the middle of a tectonic plate, far from the plate's edges and possible collisions with nearby plates. The area known as the Pacific Rim is defined by these colliding plates; along this so-called rim of fire, lofty mountain ranges like the Andes are forced up and island archipelagos like Japan and Indonesia are created. Volcanoes and earthquakes come with the package.

But Hawaii is different. Tens of millions of years ago, magma from deep in the earth's mantle bled through a thin spot in the tectonic plate that present-day Hawaii sits on. The first Hawaiian island began growing, layering itself as a shield volcano with successive and reasonably sedate eruptions over time. It finally surfaced and became an island – actually an immense, rounded mountain when measured from its base. The island's weight eventually sealed the thin spot, but the tectonic plate was, and still is, sliding northwest (perhaps four inches yearly). The hot spot burned new holes in the plate to create a successive chain of islands, and *voila*... the 132 Hawaiian islands and atolls. The city of Honolulu is 1,367 miles (2,190km) from Kure Atoll, the most northwest island of the state.

The youngest island – the Big Island – is smooth and rounded, typical of shield volcanoes. Follow the

Right: *nene,* or Hawaiian goose
Opposite: 19th century warrior

islands to the northwest where each successive island is older and more eroded – angular, lower and less massive.

The islands sat naked for a long time. Eventually, spores and seeds borne by high winds, tides, or migratory birds took root. Insects and more birds followed. There are now 10,000 insect species alone in Hawaii, nearly all unique to the islands. Each new species made itself a niche, and competition from similar species and the threat of enemies were almost non-existent. Many evolved into less defensive species; plants, for example, lost their thorns or poisonous oils. The first two mammal species, the monk seal and the hoary bat, did little to upset the balance of nature. When people came, however, they brought plants and animals that have ecologically decimated the indigenous species. As a result, little of Hawaii today is original.

Human History – Before the Europeans

Think of Hawaii, and among other things, one thinks of coconuts, banyans, banana trees, *ti* plants, bamboo, plumeria and orchids, papayas and mangoes, pineapples and taro. But none of these are Hawaiian. They were introduced by Polynesians and Europeans, along with mosquitoes, termites, fleas, cockroaches and ants, not to mention rats, dogs, pigs, and chickens. (Snakes never made it, although now and then an occasional stowaway is found in the wheel wells of incoming jumbo jets.)

The first people arrived around AD300, give or take some centuries, and probably accidentally at first, but later in continual migrations over several centuries. It is thought that they came from the Marquesas Islands, across 2,500 miles (4,023km) of open ocean in canoes. Seeking to escape domestic turmoil or population pressures, they navigated by stars and by literally

Above: new beach in making
Left: tattooed hula dancer

reading the ocean and its contours. Originally violent and cannibalistic, the newcomers settled down over four or five centuries, becoming peaceful over time. Then the Tahitians arrived around 1100. Aggressive and wanting the islands for themselves, the Tahitians conquered and enslaved the Marquesians. Tahitian migrations continued for several centuries, then ebbed and stopped. Hawaii was once again isolated. A civilization coalesced, with social, political and economic hierarchies becoming well-defined: the royal *ali`i*, the *kahuna* – the spiritual and enlightened elite – and the *maka`ainana*, or commoners.

Life was not idyllic and peaceful. The majority of people – the commoners working the land – lived under feudal conditions defined by the strict law of *kapu* – the laws of forbidden things to do, eat, see, or walk upon. Violations, however well-intentioned, were punishable by immediate death. Added to this, tribal identities were now firmly entrenched, and with it, almost continual fighting.

The Arrival of the Europeans

There is speculation that Europeans – most likely the Spanish – might have visited Hawaii before Captain James Cook. The first documented contact was made in January 1778, when Cook and his ships, the *Discovery* and the *Resolution*, skirted past Oahu before dropping anchor in Kauai's Waimea Bay. The Polynesian migrations had long ceased, and protected by geographical and cultural isolation, the *ali`i* and *kahuna* classes had established a secure power structure for themselves within their tribes. At the same time, there was constant conflict with the other tribes.

Cook's arrival upset the system in a number of ways. Most immediate was the introduction of disease to the islands; half his crew of 112 had venereal disease. Cook unsuccessfully tried to restrict his men's socializing with island women. Contrary to revisionist images of Western explorers, Cook was considered to be a decent, humane and benevolent man, fully aware, as his journals show, of the irreversible change his visits would bring throughout the Pacific.

Not only did the Hawaiians succumb to venereal disease, but also to common Western illnesses for which the Hawaiians had no immunity against. In the 50 years after Cook's arrival, the native population is estimated to have dropped from 300,000 to 60,000.

Cook's arrival on the Big Island – and his death there the following year – was witnessed by a young man. A careful observer of the Europeans and their weapons, Kamehameha – the lonely one – was a quick student. He began his conquest of Hawaii a decade later, first with rival chiefs on the Big Island, then of the neighboring islands. Taught European battle tactics by Captain George Vancouver (who was on Cook's original voyage, as was Captain Bligh, later

Above: Captain Cook arrived in Kauai in 1778

of the HMS *Bounty*), Kamehameha used a canoe-mounted cannon to conquer all the islands, save Kauai, which yielded to pragmatism years later. What motivated Kamehameha is debatable. Some call him Napoleonic, while others prefer to think of him as a visionary. Whatever it was, Hawaii experienced continual peace during Kamehameha's rule. But changes that would ultimately transform Hawaii were in the making.

Kamehameha's death in 1819 was followed quickly by the arrival of the first trade ships and whaling vessels, the fall of the *kapu* system, and the arrival of the New England missionaries.

Societies without anchors are vulnerable, and when the *kapu* system evaporated, a vacuum waited to be filled. The new missionaries obliged. Not only did they fill the spiritual vacuum, they sought to destroy or repress all aspects of Hawaiian culture, like the hula, sacred *mele* chants, the native value system, and any connection at all with the Hawaiian past before 1820.

From Whaling to Sugar

About the same time, Hawaii became an international whaling center. Whalers, expecting a lusty good time, and missionaries were often at odds; one whaling crew was so frustrated that they fired cannonballs at a preacher's new house in Lahaina. But whaling eventually died out, the whalers left, and the missionary families began to consolidate their power. Within a generation or two,

Hawaiian and Pidgin Words

No chance for us to learn Hawaiian in a short time. But there are a number of words used in daily conversation throughout the islands. Thanks to the early missionaries, Hawaiian has but 12 roman letters in its alphabet. Like Spanish, the a, e, i, o, and u vowels have only one pure sound; no lazy English vowel sounds. W confuses people: after i or e it is usually, but not always, pronounced as a v. At the start of the word, follow custom. Some Hawaiian words seem a little long, for example, humuhumunukunukuapua`a. Many long words use repeating structures. In the above word, which is a common trigger fish, humu and nuku each appear twice. So now, humu humu nuku nuku apu a`a is more manageable. But not all apparent repeating sounds are in fact that way. When in doubt, just ask. Good luck.

aloha: love, greetings, farewell
ali`i: royalty, chief
haole: outsider or foreigner, esp. Caucasian
kama`aina: local resident
keiki: child, boy or girl
kokua: help, assistance

lanai: porch, balcony
mahalo: thank you
malihini: newcomer
`ohana: family
paniolo: cowboy
pau: finished

Pidgin

There's only one rule in the speaking or pronunciation of pidgin English: don't. You'll sound quite stupid, if not ridiculous; only a local raised in Hawaii can speak pidgin properly. But it's nice to understand some of what you might hear.

beef: fight or physical disagreement
brah: brother, friend
cockaroach: steal, rip off
da kine: the thing being talked about, or when you can't think of the right word
howzit: How are you?
mo` bettah: better, something good
no can: cannot
poi dog: hound dog of indeterminate origins, mutt
stink eye: a dirty look

their names – Bishop, Campbell, Cooke, Wilcox – became synonymous with land ownership and political power. But the names of power didn't stop with the missionaries.

Businessmen and entrepreneurs replaced whalers, and they wanted land, not whales and women. The Hawaiian monarchy was pressured to recognize the

idea of land *ownership*, not the traditional Hawaiian idea of land *use*, usually decided by the king. The Great Mahele of 1848 divided the land between the monarchy, the chiefs, and the common people. The businessmen saw a certain future, and foreign ownership of land was approved two years later. The local people, still baffled by the idea of ownership, were taken for a penny.

Once land ownership became the law of the island, business and agricultural empires flourished. Sugar dominated the economy, along with export of natural resources like sandalwood to China. By the 1870s, the monarchy and resident Euro-American businessmen were jockeying for power. When the new queen, Lili`uokalani, sought to make changes to the constitution to enhance native Hawaiian power in 1891, it led to a coup d'etat by American business interests in 1893 which succeeded with the assistance of American troops landing in Honolulu.

American Territory

A republic was declared, Sanford Dole was named president (his son would make pineapples famous), and six years later, Hawaii was part of American territory. The roster of powerful family names grew: Smart, Castle, Cooke, Baldwin, Alexander, Brewer. Some of these names combined forces, eventually known as an entity called the Big Five; for example, Castle & Cooke, and Alexander & Baldwin. The Big Five, along with a number of large ranches, today own 22 percent of Hawaii – over a-third of all private property in the state.

But as the agricultural concerns gained in power and size, they needed more workers. Chinese, Japanese, Europeans and Filipinos were imported as contract workers. Over the years, many of these immigrant laborers decided to make Hawaii home. They themselves became entrepreneurs, and the power balance began to shift.

People started to marry across racial lines, hardly common anywhere in the world then. One's identity was no longer a racial one so much as it was of a group, albeit a group still defined by ethnic traditions. Too, people began to think of themselves as *American* in some ways, and with that feeling the notion of power participation and shared decision making. The ruling

Above: Queen Lili`uokalani, 1893

families lost their oligarchical omnipotence. Statehood in 1959, and the launch of jet service that year, soon made tourism Hawaii's economic engine.

Japan attacked Pearl Harbor on December 7, 1941, bringing both the United States and Hawaii into adulthood. Ironically, while thousands of Americans of Japanese ancestry (AJAs) on the mainland were imprisoned as security risks, few of the Japanese in Hawaii were persecuted, although the suspicion and rumor-mongering – in large part by mainlanders – was considerable. As a large portion of Hawaii's population was AJA, mass imprisonment was impractical. But equally important, if not more so, was that the other ethnic and cultural groups in Hawaii had no doubts about the loyalty of the AJAs. The Japanese-Americans were *kama`aina* (local residents), after all.

Some Social and Cultural Considerations

Simplifying a complex history involving numerous cultural and economic perspectives is dubious and risky. When one says *Hawaiian* today, who is one talking about? The racially-pure descendants of the early Tahitians – now numbering less than a thousand? Even that classification is questionable, given the sexual mingling that started the day Cook's ships dropped anchor in Hawaii. Or does one mean a person with the right attitude, a resident who has adapted to local ways rather than imposed outside ones? No one has a good answer, it seems, and neither do I.

Hawaii is often mentioned as an example of a truly-extraordinary co-existence of diverse cultural and ethnic interests. But racial and cultural prejudices do exist. Human nature demands such. Rarely does it exist on an individual level; usually it's more a group thing. Cultural identity in Hawaii can be strong, almost clannish; yet on the individual level, Hawaii is very tolerant and diverse. Proof is the amazingly high percentage – nearly half – of inter-racial marriages. Local folks will proudly talk of ancestry at once Chinese, Korean, Japanese, Scots, Portuguese, German and Hawaiian. While it remains true that racial attitudes are generally tolerant, since the centennial of the overthrow of the monarchy, the native Hawaiian sovereignty movement has gained numerous adherents, and credibility that has added a new and as yet undefined dynamism to the nature of the Hawaiian melting pot.

Another good example of the intermingling of races can be seen in Hawaii's

food. As various ethnic groups arrived in the Hawaiian Islands throughout history, they brought with them their culinary traditions and practices. Workers in the fields started tasting the unusual foods in each other's lunch boxes – Japanese teriyaki beef here, Korean *kim chee* there – and eventually they started borrowing ideas from each other. Today, many of Hawaii's restaurants – be they high-end Euro-Asian restaurants or no-frills plate-lunch takeaways – combine influences from the many gastronomical worlds of its varied people.

Left: tattooed local

HISTORY HIGHLIGHTS

c. AD 300–500 Polynesians discover and settle in uninhabited Hawaii.

c. 1100–1300 Tahitians arrive and over-power islands' earlier inhabitants.

c. 1400 Hawaiian society and culture develop, especially tribal and social class identities.

c. 1750 Kamehameha I born on the Big Island.

1778 Capt James Cook arrives at Waimea Bay, Kauai, with the British ships *Resolution* and *Discovery*.

1779 Capt Cook killed by Hawaiians at Kealakekua Bay, on the Big Island.

1790–95 Kamehameha I consolidates his power on the Big Island, then con-quers Maui, Lanai, Molokai, and Oahu. Kauai submits by negotiation in 1810.

1803 Kamehameha makes Lahaina his capital.

1819 Kamehameha I dies. His wife and son abolish the *kapu* system.

1820 Protestant missionaries arrive.

1835 Sugar plantation started in Kauai.

1840 Hawaii's first constitution intro-duced by Kamehameha III.

1842 United States recognizes the King-dom of Hawaii.

1845 Hawaii's capital changed from La-haina to Honolulu.

1848 Start of the 'Great Mahele', di-viding land among royalty, commoners, government, and later, foreigners.

1852 First Chinese field workers arrive.

1866 First leprosy patients forced to Kalaupapa, on Molokai.

1868 First Japanese field workers arrive.

1872 Kamehameha V dies, ending Kamehameha dynasty.

1873 Father Damien arrives at Molokai leprosy colony; dies in 1889 of leprosy.

1879 Portuguese immigrants arrive.

1891 King Kalakaua dies, succeeded by Queen Lili`uokalani.

1893 Lili`uokalani overthrown by Amer-ican businessmen. End of monarchy.

1894 US recognizes the Republic of Hawaii. Sanford Dole is made president.

1898 US annexes Hawaii.

1900 US establishes the Territory of Hawaii.

1901 Waikiki's first real hotel, the Moana, opens. Pineapples introduced as a cash crop.

1912 Duke Kahanamoku, a surfing champion, wins a gold medal for swim-ming in the Olympics.

1927 First nonstop flight to Hawaii from North America.

1935 Radio broadcast of 'Hawaii Calls' begins from the Moana Hotel.

1941 Japan attacks Pearl Harbor.

1954 Japanese-Americans, the largest minority, dominate state legislature.

1959 Hawaii becomes the 50th Amer-ican state. The first passenger jet lands.

1968 Surfing turns professional at Sun-set Beach.

1974 George Ariyoshi becomes the first Japanese-American governor in US.

1976 A double-hulled canoe, the Hokule`a, leaves Hawaii for Tahiti us-ing traditional navigation.

1982 Kauai is left devastated by Hurri-cane Iwa.

1983 Hawaii's population hits 1 million.

1986 The first ethnically-Hawaiian gov-ernor, John Waihee, takes office.

1990 Kilauea Volcano destroys Kala-pana and surrounding homes.

1993 Centennial of overthrow of the monarchy generates new interest in Hawaiian sovereignty.

1994 Filipino-American Ben Cayetano is elected the state's governor.

1997 Trustees of Bishop Estate come under scrutiny for allegations of breach-ing fiduciary responsibilities.

1998 Jack Lord, of *Hawaii Five-O*, dies in Honolulu. Ni`ihau Ranch ceases op-eration; Robinson family considers sell-ing Ni`ihau because of tax liabilities.

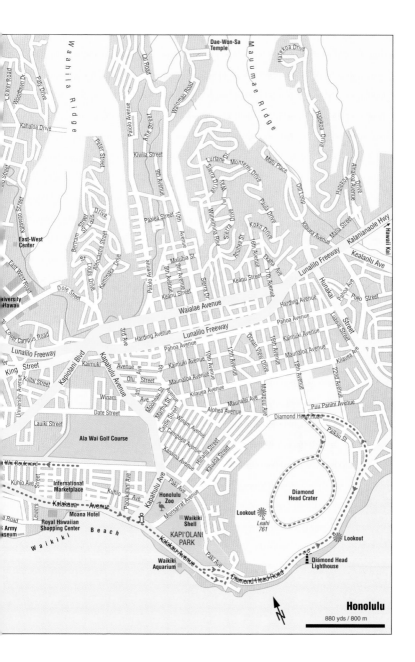

Honolulu

880 yds / 800 m

Oahu

Orientation

A curse upon you should you never leave Waikiki while on Oahu. But in fact, a large percentage of visitors do exactly just that – they don't leave Waikiki except for the airport. It's certainly a blot on their reputation as travelers, for Oahu is one of the most beautiful islands anywhere in the ocean, whether or not one likes a big city on it. If the urban hum of Honolulu upsets any preconceptions of tropical paradise, on the other side of the mountain is terrain and lifestyle as rural as anywhere in the Hawaiian islands.

But why dismiss Honolulu? It is one of the more pleasant cities anywhere – just the right size, a quirky hybrid of East and West, and with everything one needs to live well, and with enough nearby hiking trails, waterfalls, beaches and coral reefs to make any chamber of commerce whip itself into a lather. Yeah, I know, there is the traffic...

Taking the Tours

Our 2-day itinerary covers the urban and the rural sides of Oahu. *Itinerary 1* starts with a perch atop Tantalus, overlooking the city and its setting. Then you descend right into the downtown district, exploring on foot its government, history, waterfront commerce, and business. You can't miss the tall bronze statue of Duke Paoa Kahanamoku which faces Kalakaua Avenue. If modern-day Hawaii has a contemporary legend, it is the Duke, whose most enduring legacy lives on through thousands of surfers in Hawaii and all around the world. Feeling worn out after your first day in paradise? Well, an evening in bustling Waikiki will certainly keep the jet lag at bay.

Itinerary 2 circles the island, following a small road along primal cliffs, exploding waves, and rolling fields of pineapple and sugar cane. It leads to the North Shore, better known as 'the country,' with landscapes so different from those on the Honolulu side that it could pass as one of the slower-paced neighboring islands.

The following three itineraries, shorter in duration, can be added to either of the first two itineraries, done separately, or strung together. *Itinerary 3* is a short loop around Oahu's stupendous southeast end, with super beaches and lookouts. This outing could take 2 hours or all day, depending on how much of a beach bum you turn into. The Bishop Museum (*Itinerary 4*) is something of a regional Smithsonian, where you could spend hours just rambling around. The USS *Arizona* Memorial (*Itinerary 5*) is the most popular free attraction on Oahu, and requires 3 to 4 hours at least. Both the museum and memorial are centrally located.

Right: Duke Paoa Kahanamoku, father of surfing
Opposite: sundown at Waikiki

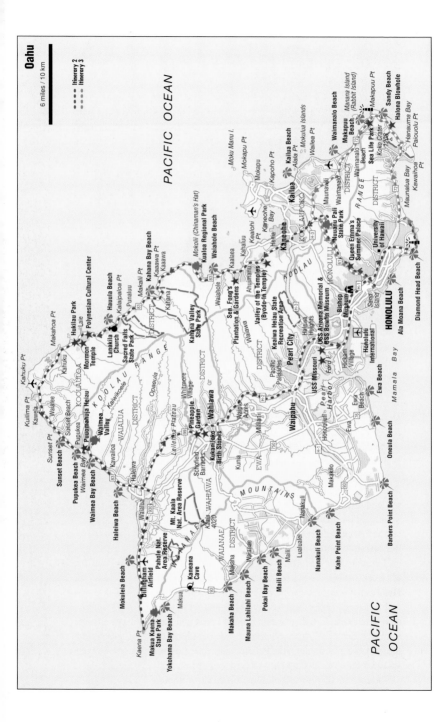

Oahu

6 miles / 10 km

···· Itinerary 2
···· Itinerary 3

PACIFIC OCEAN

PACIFIC OCEAN

Makahoa Pt
Kuilima Pt
Kahuku Pt
Kawela
Waialee
Kahuku
Sunset Beach
Sunset Pt
Pupukea
Waimea Bay
Pupukea Beach
Waimea Bay Beach
Kawailoa
Haleiwa
Kaena Pt
Mokuleia Beach
Dillingham Airfield
Pahole Nat. Area Reserve
Makua Kaena State Park
Yokohama Bay Beach
Makua
Kaneana Cave
Mt. Kaala Nat. Area Reserve
Kaala 4020
Makaha Beach
Makaha
Mauna Lahilahi Beach
Pokai Bay Beach
Maili Beach
Maili
Luualei
Nanakuli
Waianae
Waiadae
Nanakuli Beach
Kahe Point Beach
Barbers Point Beach
Oneula Beach
Ewa Beach
Ewa

Hukilau Park
Laie
Polynesian Cultural Center
Mormon Temple
Lanakila Church
Puuomahuka Heiau
Waimea Valley
Sacred Falls State Park
Punaluu
Kahana
Hauula Beach
Kalaipaloa Pt
Makalii Pt
Kaaawa Pt
Kaaawa
Kahana Bay Beach
Kahana Valley State Park
Mokolii (Chinaman's Hat)
Kualoa Regional Park
Waiahole Beach
Kaalaea
Waiahole
Waikane
Waiawa
Kahaluu
Heeia Bay
Kaneohe Bay
Kealohi Pt
Mokapu
Mokapu Pt
Moku Manu I.
Moku Manu Pt
Mokulua Islands
Kapoho Pt
Wailea Pt
Alala Pt
Kailua Beach
Kailua
Waimanalo Beach
Waimanalo
Makapuu Beach
Makapuu Pt
Mana Island (Rabbit Island)
Sandy Beach
Halona Blowhole
Halona Bay
Hanauma Bay
Paiouolo Pt
Koko Crater
Sea Life Park
Maunalua Bay
Kawaihoa Pt

Kaena Pt
Waianae
WAIANAE DISTRICT
MOUNTAINS
Kunia
Makakilo
Barbers Point Beach

Leilehua Plateau
Opaeula
Kawailoa
Whitmore
Village
Pineapple Garden
Wahiawa
Kukaniloko Birth Stones
Schofield Barracks
Wahiawa
Waipio Acres
Mililani
Waipahu
Waipio
Pearl Harbor
Ford Island
USS Arizona Memorial & USS Bowfin Museum
USS Missouri
Aiea
Pearl City
Halawa Heights
Kalauao
Pacific Palisades
Sen. Fong's Plantation & Gardens
Valley of the Temples (Byodo-In Temple)
Ahuimanu
Kaneohe
Keaiwa Heiau State Recreation Area
Bishop Museum
HONOLULU
Hickam Village
Honolulu International
Ala Moana Beach
Sand Island
Diamond Head Beach
University of Hawaii
Queen Emma's Summer Palace
Nuuanu Pali State Park
Maunawili
Waimanalo

KOOLAU RANGE
KOOLAU DISTRICT
WAHIAWA DISTRICT
EWA DISTRICT
KOOLAUPOKO
KOOLAU RANGE
HONOLULU DISTRICT

Mamala Bay

oahu

1: HONOLULU AND WAIKIKI AREA *(see maps, p18 & p24)*

A first day in paradise – breakfast on the beach, followed by a ramble around Honolulu, the capital city. Lofty views, Hotel Street, Chinatown, the waterfront, America's only royal palace, parks and shopping, and, of course, Waikiki.

Outwit any pesky jet lag with a dawn ocean swim along Waikiki Beach, followed by a grand breakfast. This first Hawaiian breakfast must be proper – outside and embraced by the tropical morning. Trust me – there's no better way in Waikiki to baptize the day than from a table at **Orchids**, at the regal-like **Halekulani Hotel**, watching Diamond Head wake up. Alternatively, try an outside table at the **Banyan Veranda**, at the **Sheraton Moana-Surfrider** (c. 1901), Waikiki's first hotel.

By car, follow Ala Wai Boulevard to McCully Street. The smooth waters of the Ala Wai Canal – built during the 1920s to empty the fishponds taro fields and marsh now called Waikiki – ripple gently during outrigger canoe club practices. Follow McCully, then take a left into South Beretania Street, just before McCully arches into an overpass. Make a right into Punahou Street, but before it begins climbing into Manoa Valley, turn left into Nehoa Street, then right into Makiki Street.

Round Top Drive spirals upwards through a residential area, breaking out at a lookout with prime vistas towards Diamond Head and Waikiki. **Diamond Head** is a tuff cone, popping up about 150,000 years ago through the coral reef in a set of violent steam explosions. The ocean side of Diamond Head, arching upward, is higher because the northeast trade winds deposited more ash there. Directly below you, the lush and wet **Manoa Valley** opens from the Ko'olau Mountains; the 20,000-student University of Hawaii campus sprawls at the valley's mouth.

The road climbs further up **Tantalus** to **Pu`u`ualaka`a State Wayside Park**, nice for a short walk and still another stupendous view, this time extending from left of Diamond Head to Ewa. Notice that what you see is

Above: downtown Honolulu

mostly flat, including downtown Honolulu. This is what geologists call a coral bench, formed when the sea level was 25ft (7.5m) higher.

Continue up Tantalus through deep and lush rainforest, circling around for several miles before descending into **Punchbowl Crater**. Inside this tuff cone is the **National Memorial Cemetery of the Pacific**. The Hawaiian name for Punchbowl is Puowaina – hill of sacrifice. The Punchbowl Lookout offers a panoramic view of the city and the Ko`olau Mountains.

Zigzag from Queen Emma Street to Vineyard Boulevard to Punchbowl Street. It's time for a walk. Suggested parking: left on King Street from Punchbowl, bearing left at the signal on Alapai Street and back again towards the mountains. Just before the Beretania Street signal is a nearly-camouflaged public lot; quarters are needed for the hungry 3-hour meter.

Find the **State Capitol Building**, with its tall slender pillars lifting the building above an open courtyard. On Beretania Street side is a bronze **statue of Father Damien**, priest to the Molokai leprosy colony. It faces **Washington Place**, built in 1846 by Queen Lili`uokalani's husband's family and now home to Hawaii's governor. Walk down Richards Street, then right onto Hotel Street.

Although urban renewal has gentrified portions of **Hotel Street**, some parts remain a rowdy strip, a contemporary off-shoot of the not-so-distant days when sailors on shore leave swarmed its sidewalks. Proceeding down Hotel Street you'll reach Chinatown.

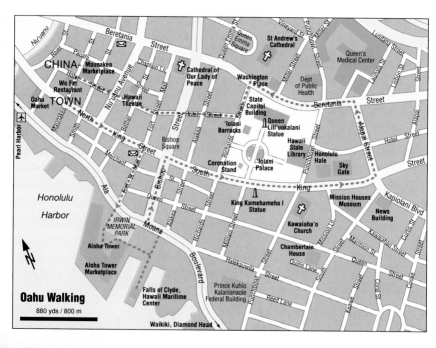

Oahu Walking

880 yds / 800 m

oahu

Chinatown

Despite burning down twice – in 1886, and again in 1900 to fight a bubonic plague epidemic – Chinatown is thick with old buildings, the stand-out being **Wo Fat**, a landmark Chinese restaurant built in 1936. At Maunakea Street is **Maunakea Marketplace**, a cluster of stores and restaurants marked by a clock tower with Chinese numbers.

Left down Maunakea Street, then left on King Street, all the while poking through vegetable stalls, acupuncture clinics, herbalists, noodle factories, antique stores and hole-in-the-wall eateries. Turn left on Bethel Street for a glimpse of the beautifully restored Hawaii Theatre, which opened in 1927.

Follow the **Fort Street Mall** straight down to the waterfront. Since 1926, the 184-ft (56-m) **Aloha Tower** has been the polestar of Honolulu's waterfront. The tower once greeted tourists arriving by boat, as did long waits in the cavernous processing area at the tower's base. Now it presides over **Aloha Tower Marketplace**, a complex of shops and restaurants.

From the tower, it's 5 minutes to the **Falls of Clyde**, built in 1878 and used as a passenger ship between Honolulu and San Francisco. Definitely visit the **Hawaii Maritime Center**, with eclectic and informative displays, from whales to surfboards to ancient canoes.

Bishop Street leads back downtown, dominated by banks and corporate loftiness. Turn right on King Street to the **King Kamehameha I statue** – look for the flock of tourists. Don't be fooled by substitutions. This is a duplicate; the original statue stands on the Big Island. Commissioned to celebrate the centennial of Captain Cook's arrival in Hawaii, the original sank near the Falkland Islands en route from Europe. A duplicate was cast, and the original later recovered. Opposite the monument is `Iolani Palace, completed in 1882 by King Kalakaua after his European travels. From 1893 until 1969, after the monarchy's fall, the palace was the capitol building for the republic, territory, and finally the state.

Further down King Street are the interesting **Mission Houses Museum** and **Kawaiaha`o Church**. The restored homes portray missionary life in the early 1800s; Kawaiaha`o Church was built in 1842 of coral cut from ocean reefs. Behind the tall dull-grey municipal building across King Street is the parking garage. On the way, state law requires you to lay down underneath the **Sky Gate** sculpture, by Isamu Noguchi, and stare at the clouds.

To Waikiki

By car, loop back around to Punchbowl Street and continue to Ala Moana Boulevard. Follow Ala Moana towards Waikiki, passing a succession of shopping centers, including the **Ward Center** complex, with its upscale shops, restaurants, and Farmer's Market. **Ala Moana Shopping Center**, the *ali`i* of Hawaii shopping centers, still growing and selling anything from plate lunches to unpronounceable Italian designer shoes.

Right: Aloha Tower
Opposite: Maunakea Marketplace

Opposite Ala Moana Shopping Center is **Ala Moana Beach Park** and **Aina Moana State Recreation Area** (locals call Aina Moana 'Magic Island'). This is a wonderful place, a cultural theater of people at play. Walk out to the end of Magic Island for mesmerizing views of the yacht harbor, Waikiki, and Diamond Head. The late afternoon light casts a special atmospheric magic here.

Waikiki, a place to love and hate at the same time. Somehow it all works – the hotels, condominiums, shopping arcades, restaurants, movie theaters and the beach. And even more, it's got the best people-watching anywhere, with resplendent sunsets to boot. Five minutes by foot towards Diamond Head is the 200-plus-acre (69-ha) **Kapi`olani Park**, embracing a zoo, aquarium, weekend art festivals, the perpetual **Kodak Hula Show**, an outdoor concert venue (**Waikiki Shell**) and plenty of open space for playing.

Drive around Diamond Head, past the lighthouse and bronzed surfers in the water below, and drive straight into the crater from around back. A trail and stairs lead to the 761-ft (232-m) summit.

Twilight Stroll

Eventually sunset beckons you to settle down. Nearly anywhere in Waikiki is good. For a proper drink and *pupus* with sunset, return to your breakfast spot at either the Halekulani or the Sheraton Moana-Surfrider. The Halekulani's **House Without a Key** is a great place to enjoy Hawaiian music, hula and 'heavy pupus,' that can easily serve as dinner, while more formal dining is offered at **Orchids** or **La Mer**. Try the **Parc Cafe** at the Waikiki Parc Hotel for its delightful buffet, or stop by **Keo's** for great Thai food.

Wandering along Waikiki's **Kalakaua Avenue** at twilight is a wonderful experience. It's perfect place for a spontaneous stroll. Detailed Waikiki walking itineraries always fail dismally. But some recommendations: the **Historical Room** of the Sheraton Moana-Surfrider; the sunset **torchlighting ceremony** at the Diamond Head-end of Waikiki Beach, across from the Hyatt Regency; the shops and entertainment at the **Royal Hawaiian Shopping Center**, and the **International Marketplace** for an outdoor bazaar where bargaining is *de rigeur*; or simply the beach itself.

Above: Kodak Hula Show

2: ISLAND CIRCLE – WINDWARD AND NORTH SHORE
(see map, p22)

A circular drive around Hawaii's most under-appreciated island. See the world's most famous surfing area and a sacrificial heiau, then enjoy an evening among the stars, both literally and figuratively.

There are three routes from Honolulu through the Ko`olau Mountains to the windward side: H3 through Halawa, Likelike Highway or the Pali Highway. Take the latter

Seconds after getting on the Pali from the H1 freeway, look out on your right for the **Honpa Hongwanji Mission**, a Buddhist temple impossible to miss. Beyond, the highway climbs steadily up **Nu`uanu Valley**. Just before the top and the first of two short tunnels, pull off for **Nu`uanu Pali State Park**. The Ko`olau Range is the remnant of Oahu's younger of two extinct volca-

noes. The Honolulu side is the exterior slope, gradual and corrugated with valleys. The windward side is the crater's interior, with cliffs rising up to 3,000ft (915m). Looking windward from the Pali overlook, **Kane`ohe** is left, **Kailua** is right and near the old volcano's eruptive center. The spire across the way is the 1,643-ft (501-m) Olomana Peak, a stubborn caldera dike.

In 1795, during his Oahu conquest, Kamehameha I elbowed a group of defending warriors right over the cliff near the lookout. Ponder over that while descending towards Kailua the slow and safe way. At the bottom is a signal. Don't go straight, which leads to Kailua or southeast Oahu (see *Itinerary 3*). Rather, turn left on Route 83 and proceed through Kane`ohe, which has nothing to offer you except **Byodo-In**, in the Valley of the Temples along Route 83. It's a beautiful replica of a temple in Japan; this one was built in 1968 to commemorate the centennial of Hawaii's first Japanese immigrants.

Under the Ironwood Trees

Stay on Route 83 northwards, snuggling the shoreline through primal-looking terrain. The drive is rural and quiet, with several pleasant stops along the way. **Kualoa Regional Park**, with a sensational beach, is opposite **Chinaman's Hat**, properly called Mokoli`i. **Kahana Bay Beach Park**, backed by the rainforest of **Kahana Valley State Park**, is a tranquil stop for a picnic or an earnest snooze beneath whispering ironwood trees. Another excellent alternative further is **Malaekahana Bay State Recreation Area**, with good snorkeling and gentle waters.

You've seen the ubiquitous advertisements, now see the real thing (well, maybe): the **Polynesian Cultural Center**, owned and operated

Above: Byodo-In temple
Right: beach paradise

by the Mormon church. Clearly, many visitors enjoy the somewhat Disneyland approach to Pacific island cultures. The staffers are all islanders (students from neighboring Brigham Young University's Hawaii campus), full of contagious good spirits, and well-versed in the seven island cultures they represent. No, it's not like going to Tahiti or Samoa or New Zealand, and the playful interactive chatter with visitors may be a bit predictable. But it can nonetheless be fun despite such obvious limitations.

It's only a short drive from the Center to Laie's **Mormon Temple**, which welcomes visitors. A few miles further on you'll reach Kahuku, a quiet ex-plantation town that now serves as a center of Hawaiian aquaculture. You'll see the prawn farms and can make a lunch stop at the roadside truck that serves them up. The **Turtle Bay Hilton**, one of Oahu's two destination resorts (the other is Ko Olina on the leeward side) is nearby. Sunday brunch is a gala here, and there's golf, horseback riding and miles of uncrowded beach that may make a stop worthwhile, but the hotel itself is in definite need of an upgrade.

Surf's Up

And now the **North Shore**, surf capital of known galaxy. Somewhere along 2-mile (3-km) long **Sunset Beach** is the infamous Banzai Pipeline. It's not marked, but scores of surfers coasting along the road know *exactly* where it is. Ask. If it's summertime, you'll wonder what the fuss is all about, as there's probably hardly a ripple, much less a wave, in sight. Come back in winter when waves reach 30ft (9m), even higher to the west.

Even more radical waves break at **Waimea Bay**. But just before Waimea, turn left at the Foodland grocery store, climbing the road to the **Pu`uomahuka Heiau** turnoff. This is the largest heiau, a large open-air temple, on Oahu. One can only hope that the view mellowed the misery of sacrificial victims in 1792, among them some hapless British sailors.

Behind Waimea Bay and the beach, a road leads to **Waimea Valley**, an archeologically important site surrounded by 1,800 acres of nature preserve accessed by mountain bike, all terrain vehicle, on foot, or by a jitney that links various sites in the valley.

Head for **Hale`iwa**, the North Shore's center for local commerce and tourism. On weekends, heavy traffic makes a North Shore drive slow. Get out of the car if the traffic gets to you: there are plenty of places to shop. For the hungry: fish and ocean views at **Jameson's by the Sea**; local atmosphere and hearty meals at **Cafe Haleiwa**, especially

Above: Waimea Falls; **left:** surf-seeker
Opposite: sacred Kukaniloko stone

for breakfasts that are famous island-wide; coffee, pastries and deli meals at **Coffee Gallery**, tucked away in the North Shore Marketplace, south of town.

An option: Continue along the coast to Mokule`ia Beach and Dillingham Airfield for exhilarating **glider rides**, or to the end of the road for ½-hour-long walk to **Ka`ena Point**, Oahu's western tip. In winter, 30-ft (9-m) high waves explode offshore. It's believed that the spirits of the dead come here to depart earth, so watch your step.

Pineapples and Pearl Harbor

From Hale`iwa, proceed along Route 99 south, inland through a broad valley between the Ko`olau and Wai`anae mountains. Fields of sugar cane and pineapple blanket the valley's red soil. There are no bargains at the touristy Dole Pineapple Pavilion (not even a lousy sample), but the adjacent topiary maze, the largest in the world by Guinness reckoning, is a fun diversion if you're traveling with kids. There's also an interesting pineapple garden here – at the intersection with Route 801 – the **Del Monte pineapple garden**. Then follow the intersection's left fork a bit to a signal: left leads to Whitmore Village and right empties into a field of pineapple plants, where there is a grove of tall trees. Here you'll find the **Kukaniloko Birth Stones**, marked with petroglyphs and once used by *ali`i* for giving birth.

Interstate H2 empties you onto Interstate H1 – towards Honolulu – right above **Pearl Harbor**. Consider stopping at the USS Arizona Memorial Visitor Center (see *Itinerary 5*) here. Interstate H1 also passes the Bishop Museum (see *Itinerary 4*).

Hit the beach or park, or return to the hotel. Rest up, freshen up, and then saddle up again. Drive around the front of Diamond Head to the **Kahala Mandarin Oriental**, noting some of the jillion-dollar estates along Kahala Avenue. Opened in 1964 as the Kahala Hilton, the hotel has been renovated to the tune of millions of dollars and continues to be a peerless and serene retreat. Head back to Waikiki for one of the shows on the strip: the venerable Don Ho still wows 'em at the Waikiki Beachcomber. The exciting Magic of Polynesia is a Vegas-style mix of illusion and kitschy Hawaiiana. Creation, A Polynesian Odyssey at the Princess Kaiulani features a more culturally authentic look at Hawaiian song and dance.

3: SOUTHEAST OAHU LOOP *(see map, p22)*

A short trip around Oahu's southeast tip, which has some of the island's best beaches and best views. Can be driven in a couple hours, or extended to half a day with beach time.

Don't start this excursion in late afternoon, as rush hour traffic goes in the same direction

From Waikiki follow Kalakaua Avenue through Kapi`olani Park to Diamond Head Road, continuing around Diamond Head where Diamond Head Road becomes Kahala Avenue. Follow Kahala Avenue to Hunakai Street, turn left, then right on Kilauea Avenue, past the Kahala Mall to the elevated section of the H1 Interstate, which terminates here. Turn right, which leads to the Kalanianaole Highway, heading east.

After several bedroom suburbs, the road climbs up and left. At the crest on the right is the road down to **Hanauma Bay**. It's a popular place with visitors, to the extent that it is now overused and on the threshold of ecological degradation. The state has had to restrict access and initiate a small entrance fee, and few locals visit it because of the intense crowds – as many as 10,000 people visit the bay daily. I strongly advise admiring it from up on top. There's a huge ocean around Oahu with lots of other places to play. *Let Hanauma Bay rest.*

The coast beyond Hanauma Bay is rugged, sculpted, and dramatic – testimony to the ocean's erosive power on the islands. The **Halona Blowhole** – where water is

Above: in search of seclusion
Below: boogie-boarding at Sandy Beach

forced up geyser-like through a hole in the basalt when the incoming sea swell pushes up through its underwater entrance – is popular with the tour bus circuit. Just beyond, the road flattens out. That big beach is **Sandy Beach**, one of Oahu's most popular beaches. It's also a dangerous beach at times; the unique conditions that make it a superb board and body surfing place make it tricky for the swimmer. Before going in the water, check with the lifeguards.

To the Lighthouse

The next stop is at the top of the **Makapu`u Lookout**. It's easy to zip right past the overlook when cresting the top as the view is a stunner. Looking straight up Oahu's windward coast, the lookout is one of Hawaii's best. For even better views, the **Makapu`u Lighthouse** stands tall on the top of the point. The one-mile climb up Lighthouse Road leads to lighthouse lookouts with panoramic views of mountains and sea, turtles and winter whales, islands and beaches. No restrooms, no food concession, often not that many people. Just you and nature. **Makapu`u Beach** is known for its sometimes brutal, bodysurfing waves. Across from Makapu`u is **Sea Life Park**, whose attractions include porpoise shows, hammer-head sharks, the Pacific Whaling Museum, touch pools for children, a rehabilitation center for injured monk seals, and a 300,000-gallon (1.1 million liters) simulated reef tank. There are Humboldt penguins too.

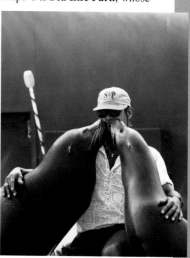

Three miles (5km) north is the town of **Waimanalo**, an exceedingly local outpost of rural Hawaii on an increasingly urban island. In the top ranks of sumo in Japan are several wrestlers, or *rikishi,* from Hawaii, including Sal Atisanoe, who wrestles as Konishiki and is from the Wai`anae coast, and Akebono, a grand champion, or *yokozuna,* from Waimanalo and known locally at Chad Rowan. Typically overlooked by nearly everyone except the locals is **Waimanalo Beach**, one of the longest and nicest white sand beaches anywhere. It's nearly empty on weekdays, but it's not exactly a paradise for naive visitors. Be sure to lock the car before hitting the beach.

Depending on the season, you'll see vendors selling everything from fresh fish and seafood to corn, mangoes and papayas. Continue past the needle-like peak of Olomana , the remnants of a volcanic dike from the old Ko`olau caldera located here over 2 million years ago. On the left is the intersection with Route 61. Right leads to the town of Kailua, a prime bedroom community for Honolulu commuters and which is also a haven for windsurfers. Left on Route 61 returns us to Honolulu. Just before it starts climbing to Nu`uanu Pali, a junction to Route 83 connects us with *Itinerary 2,* continuing north along the coast.

Above: Sea Life Park seals

4: BISHOP MUSEUM

A world-class museum and scientific institution. It's no simple boast to call the Bishop Museum the Pacific's equal to the Smithsonian. Highly recommended.

The **Bishop Museum** (1525 Bernice Street, tel: 847 3511) is a regional museum and research institute on par with the Smithsonian Institution in Washington, D C. And like the Smithsonian, hours and hours can be spent exploring the Bishop. For this reason, I've recommended it as a separate option rather than trying to squeeze it into another full itinerary.

Founded in 1889 by Charles Reed Bishop, the museum was originally built as a memorial to his wife – the last direct descendant of the Kamehameha dynasty, Princess Bernice Pauahi. Her personal collection family heirlooms were the museum's first holdings, but in the 100 years since, the collection has expanded to comprise Oceania's finest specimens, both natural and human-made. Its collection is comprehensive and even overwhelming: some 200,000 Hawaiian and Pacific artifacts; 6,000,000 shells; 250,000 plant specimens; and 13,500,000 insect specimens.

The Bishop Museum supports and coordinates extensive archeological and sociological research throughout the Pacific. Only a small portion of both this and its full collection is on display. Nonetheless, the displays are formidable, especially in the cavernous *koa*-paneled Hawaiian Hall (1903) which houses carved and feathered icons, capes and other remnants of pre-contact Hawaii.

Other visitor possibilities include craft demonstrations, a planetarium, library and archives, and Shop Pacifica. The museum is open 9am to 5pm daily. The admission fee includes entry to the Planetarium shows at 11am and 2pm, Friday and Saturday evenings at 7pm; reservations required for evening shows.

5: WORLD WAR II COMMEMORATED

Take a boat out to the memorial, built over the sunken hull of the USS
Arizona. Pay a walk-through visit of Bowfin Submarine, and then ex-
plore the Battleship Missouri. Plan a full day if you want to do it all.

The USS **Arizona Memorial** commemorates the December 7, 1941, Japanese
attack on Pearl Harbor. Over 1,000 sailors died on the *Arizona*, when a series of Japanese torpedoes and aerial bombs sank the battleship in less than

10 minutes. The remains of many are
still entombed in the hull visible from
the memorial. Often there is a wait
for the launch to the memorial.

Next door to the *Arizona* visitor center is the privately-owned USS **Bowfin
Submarine Museum**, which is highly
recommended. A genuine diesel-elec-
tric World War II submarine, the
Bowfin was credited with sinking 44
ships during its nine patrols. A huge
museum traces submarine history from
1914 to the nuclear submarine age.

A shuttle links the Bowfin museum to the **Battleship Missouri**, docked
off Ford Island, which is linked to Oahu by a bridge that crosses Pearl Harbor's East Loch. It was aboard the *Missouri*, on September 2, 1945, that
General Douglas MacArthur officially accepted the surrender of the Japanese
military, signing the armistice that ended World War II. You can wander
the decks of this venerable battleship.

USS Arizona Memorial
1 Arizona Memorial Place, Honolulu 96818, tel: 422 0561
Open daily 7.30am to 5pm. Free. Last program begins at 3pm. First come,
first served.

USS Bowfin Submarine Museum & Park
11 Arizona Memorial Drive, Honolulu 96818
Tel: 423 1341
Open daily 8am to 5pm. Admission fee for submarine and museum. Chil-
dren under four are not allowed on the
Bowfin, but most welcome in the museum.

Battleship Missouri Memorial
11 Arizona Memorial Drive
Honolulu 96818
Tel: 455 1600; advance bookings
Tel: 973 9825
Admission fee includes the shuttle from the
Bowfin Submarine Museum to the Missouri
Memorial. Open daily 8am to 5pm.

Above: Arizona Memorial; **right:** vet's salute
Opposite: inside the Bishop Museum

Orientation

The Big Island, just as promised... Twice as big as all the other Hawaiian islands combined. Geologically the youngest of the Hawaiian islands, the Big Island is actually just the above-water tip of the planet's biggest mountain, Mauna Loa, and its tallest mountain, Mauna Kea – measured from their bases. And the island still grows. Two active volcanoes punctuate the island, and a new subterranean island gestates 20 miles (32km) offshore.

Of all the Hawaiian islands, the Big Island is the most accessible for ancient Hawaiian history: temples, footpaths, petroglyphs and villages are numerous. Indeed, the Big Island was historically pivotal: it was the first landfall of venturing Polynesians from Tahiti, the last landfall of adventurous Captain Cook from England, and the point of departure for the conquest and unification of all Hawaii by Kamehameha I. It was also the latter's birthplace. The Kamehameha the Great statue at Kapa`au in North Kohala commemorates him and is, incidentally, the original statue that was once lost at sea off the Falklands Islands and later recovered.

Taking the Tours

Hilo, the state's largest city outside Oahu, hardly seems metropolitan, fortunately, but it's usually ignored by the visitor, unfortunately – Kona and Kohala, the Big Island's center of tourism and play, get all the attention and most of the sunshine. Sun-washed Kona, once the playground of Hawaiian royalty, is today crowded with boutiques, hotels, condominiums, and tourists. But while Hilo is on the island's wet side, don't let that put you off. Much of its charm originates in its quiet, unassuming residents.

The Big Island is small enough to drive around in a day, but big enough to make the journey thoroughly unsatisfying. Just as you wouldn't try 15 European cities in 10 days, don't try the Big Island in one.

While the full-day tours (see *Itineraries 6* and *7*) itinerary pivot on a night or two in South Kohala or Kona, the dry and sunny side where most hotels are located, try to extend one of the shorter options (see *Itineraries 8* and *9*) and stay the second night in Hilo or Volcano, 30 minutes from one another. Save driving time and fly out of Hilo instead of Kona. Hilo and Hawaii Volcanoes National Park are separate options that can be added to the full-day itineraries if you're pressed for time: Hilo to *Itinerary 6* and the park to *Itinerary 7*.

However, the volcanoes park really deserves a full day or better yet, three or four. And wet as it is, slow-paced Hilo, about a ½-hour's drive to the north-east and the island's seat of government, is one of my favorite parts of Hawaii simply because it's comfortable just being itself.

Right: King Kamehameha's statue at Kapa`au
Opposite: waves on soldified lava

6: KOHALA AND KONA *(see map, p38)*

Drive to the northern tip: a sacred temple, a king's birthplace, a commoners' fishing village. Cowboy country. The west coast: museum-quality art and classy resorts, petroglyphs, royal fishponds. Downtown Kona and a sunset.

Daybreak. Clear the mind with a glass of fresh orange juice. Unfold the map and trace Route 19 north along the Big Island's western coast to North Kohala. If you've decided to add the Hilo option (see *Itinerary 8*) for a long day, finish the juice and hit the road. Otherwise, sure, order another glass.

From Kona, it's an extra 30-minute drive than from the Kohala resorts. The highway traverses miles of lava flows, most recently from 1859. Just north of the Kona airport, the exclusive and uniquely reactionary **Kona Village Resort** (no televisions, telephones, or air-conditioning amidst otherwise luxurious pampering) nestles down on the coast, where Hawaii's most intimate *luau* fires up on Friday nights. In contrast, next door is the new and very upscale **Four Seasons Hualalai**. Further along, North Kona yields to South Kohala and a string of resorts and golf courses. At the junction leading to North Kohala's west coast, stop at the **Pu`ukohola Heiau**, a national historic site. Dedicated to the war god, it was built by Kamehameha I in 1791.

Follow Route 270 past Kawaihae, a utilitarian commercial port and the site where Kamehameha's war canoes set off for conquest. **Lapakahi State Historical Park** is a look back into the past of 600 years ago; in the early morning coolness it's a satisfying self-guiding walk through this stone ghost town of a commoners' fishing village.

The road ascends inland over increasingly green hills. Take the **Upolu Point** turnoff, where a modest straight-arrow road leads (after a left at the airstrip) to a passable – except when wet – dirt road to the **Mo`okini Heiau**, a temple

Above: fascinating Puako petroglyphs at Kohala

still maintained by a *kahuna* from the Mo`okini family, *heiau* guardians for perhaps 1,000 years. Nearby is **Kamehameha's Birthplace**, c. 1752. Signs mark both the heiau and the birthplace.

The main road takes you through Hawi, a one-time sugar boom town. In Hawi, sign on with the Kohala Mountain Kayak Cruise (8.15am and 12.15pm, daily) for a 3-hour excursion via the irrigation ditch that carries water from the otherwise inaccessible wilderness of the Kohala Mountains. Kayaks spend over an hour in the ditch before stopping for a swim at a waterfall-fed pool and the return to Hawi.

From Hawi head to Kapa`au, where the original **King Kamehameha statue** stands before the unassuming civic center. Refuel with a tofu burger and some wicked chocolate pie from **Don's Family Deli**. At the road's end is the **Pololu Valley Lookout**, teasing visitors with peeks of sheer ocean cliffs and a black-sand beach below. Return towards Hawi but don't blink or you'll miss it on the left: the **Kohala Tong Wo Society building**. Founded in 1886, it's the last of many Chinese societies established on the Big Island. Admire it from the road; it's private property. Look inside **Ackerman Gallery** in Kapa`au before turning south onto Route 250, which climbs Kohala Mountain, residue of an extinct volcano. Spectacular views – if the vog, or volcanic smog, isn't thick – of Mauna Kea (13,677ft/4,168m) and Mauna Loa (13,679ft/4,169m) unfold as the road descends to Waimea.

Rustic Waimea

Waimea retains its rustic ranch town feel despite recent gentrification and a shift from ranching as the only game in town, although the Parker Ranch, said to be the largest individually-held ranch in America, is still the dominant economic force. Don't be confused by Waimea's several names. The post office calls the town Kamuela, to distinguish it from Waimea on Kaua`i. Road signs however say Waimea, as do residents. In town, the **Edelweiss** and **Merriman's**, both started by culinary escapees from Kohala resorts, are island classics for lunch and dinner.

Should the siren call of beach-time summon, it's but a short drive back to South Kohala and Kona. Otherwise, continue east on Route 19 to Honoka`a and the **Waipi`o Valley Lookout**, 1,000ft (305m) above this huge transcendent valley. Once a powerful social and cultural focal point, it was inhabited by thousands of people for at least a millennium.

Unless you've decided to make a run for Hilo this afternoon, return back through Waimea. I always stop at the **Kamuela Museum**, on the west side of town. It's like a person's attic put on public display. Vietcong flags share display cases with Chinese antiques.

Returning to South Kohala, consider a visit to the **Mauna Kea Beach Hotel**, grand-daddy

Right: Waimea rodeo

of the Kohala resorts. Its Asian and Pacific art collection is magnificent, as is its crescent beach. Next door is the newer **Hapuna Beach Prince Hotel**, which sprawls across a bluff above the beach and commands ocean views from here to eternity. Down the coast is the **Mauna Lani Bay Hotel & Bungalows**, which I think is the finest Kohala resort. (Don't be fooled by its lack

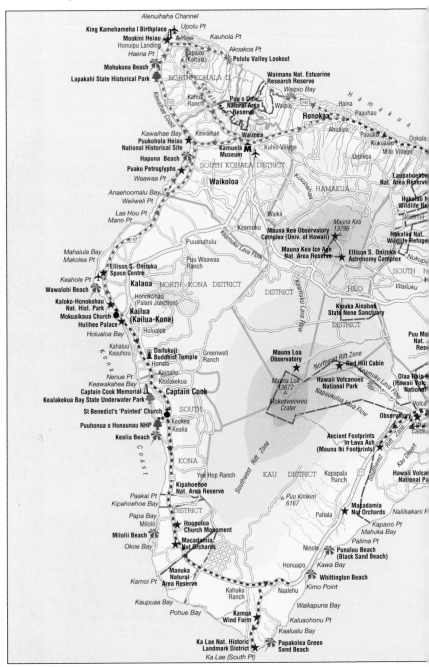

of theatrics so rampant in newer 'fantasy' resorts. Likewise, don't be fooled by 'bungalows,' if memories of beach bungalows in Thailand or Fiji return; these cost US$2,500 a night.) Explore footpaths around ancient fishponds and shelter caves. Highly recommended are any of its restaurants.

Returning towards the highway, follow the signs to the **Puako petroglyph fields**, where you will find examples of the fascinating ancient rock drawings which represent scenes of life in pre-contact Hawaii. Further down the coast, another well-marked, 1,000-year-old petroglyph field is at the Waikoloa Resort complex. The **Outrigger Waikoloan Resort** has well-preserved ancient fishponds.

Late afternoon. Where to settle in for sunset? **Hapuna Beach**, the island's largest white-sand beach, is perfect.

Or head to **Kailua-Kona**. Known to locals as Kona, the post office as Kailua-Kona, and shown on maps as Kailua, the leeward side's largest town is the island's social hot spot. Park near the harbor. **King Kamehameha's Kona Beach Hotel**, situated at the king's royal compound during the last decade of his life, offers tours of the grounds. Walk along Ali`i Drive towards the **Royal Kona Resort**, obvious across the harbor and Kona's best place to stay. Midway is **Moku`aikaua Church**, built in 1837.

Sunset is free along the harbor seawall or on the pier. Add dinner to the view at **Jameson's By The Sea** or **Huggo's**, both located on Ali`i Drive. For fine dining, try the **La Bourgogne** at the Kuakini Plaza.

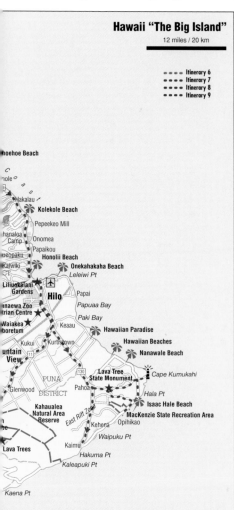

Hawaii "The Big Island"

12 miles / 20 km

- - - - Itinerary 6
- - - - Itinerary 7
- - - - Itinerary 8
- - - - Itinerary 9

hoehoe Beach

Coast

nole

Hakalau

Kolekole Beach

Pepeekeo Mill

hanaloa Camp   Onomea

Papaikou

ueopaku   Honolii Beach

Kaiwiki   Onekahakaha Beach

Leleiwi Pt

Liliuokalani Gardens

Hilo   Papai

naewa Zoo trian Centre   Papuaa Bay

Paki Bay

Waiakea boretum   Keaau   Hawaiian Paradise

Kukui   Kurtistown   Hawaiian Beaches

untain View   Nanawale Beach

Lava Tree State Monument   Cape Kumukahi

PUNA   Pahoa   Hala Pt

Glenwood   DISTRICT

Isaac Hale Beach

Kahaualea Natural Area Reserve   MacKenzie State Recreation Area

East Rift Zone   Kehena   Opihikao

Lava Trees   Kaimu   Waipuku Pt

Hakuma Pt

Kaleapuki Pt

Kaena Pt

PACIFIC OCEAN

7: SOUTH KONA AND SOUTH POINT *(see map, p38)*

Breakfast in a theater. Lots of chocolate brownies. A sacred place of refuge. The end of Captain Cook. An old hotel with great pork chops. Coffee beans. America's southernmost point. Thirty-six windmills.

Of course... Do order that freshly-squeezed orange juice, but skip breakfast. A better idea waits elsewhere. Yesterday you went north until there was no more. Today it's south until the same.

From Kona, follow Route 11 towards Honalo, Kainaliu, and Kealakekua, clustered near the bigger town of Captain Cook and nearly impossible for the visitor to tell apart. Note **Teshima's** in Honalo on the left; it's not worth a special drive, but if in the area later and hungry, give it a try for pure local atmosphere. A breakfast worth the drive is waiting for you at the **Aloha Theater Cafe**, in Kainaliu. Food any time of the day is good and tempting (but skip the croissants), especially when eaten on the outside terrace. Check the community theater schedule then buy a big bag of their delicious brownies for the road. Down the road in the town of **Captain Cook** proper is the **Manago Hotel** on the right, where the menu is simple and cheap, and known for its lip-smacking pork chops. The Manago family has owned and operated the hotel for over 70 years. Rooms are basic but quiet.

Makai of town – towards the ocean – is **Kealakekua Bay**, a state marine conservation district and the site of Captain Cook's 1779 dismemberment by insulted Hawaiians. If time allows later, consider snorkeling here. There's a *heiau* and an inaccessible 27-ft (8-m) high white monument on British territory solemnizing Cook. For now, pass on by.

Coffee Country

All along the highway south of Kona, in the small villages clustered around Captain Cook, Kona coffee is sold. But there is no urgent need to buy it here, as bean prices are reasonably consistent from island to island. But it's definitely freshest here. Forget the blends – they're only 10 percent pure Kona.

Take the turnoff to **Pu`uhonua o Honaunau National Historical Park**, called the 'city of refuge' by the lazy. Meticulously and accurately restored, it was indeed an ancient refuge where transgressors and *kapu* violators were pardoned by priests – but only after outswimming sharks or scaling stone walls, and vowing to do penance. This *pu`uhonua* gained increasing spiritual power, or *mana*, over the centuries as the final resting place of the bones of Kona's high-born chiefs. When the *kapu* system collapsed in 1819, so

Above: inside St Benedict's Church

did the *pu`uhonua's* importance. The guided tours are highly recommended, and the grounds themselves are wonderful for idle walking, simple day-dreaming, or inspections of the full-sized primitive idols and the 1,000-ft (305-m) long, 10-ft (3-m) high and 17-ft (5½-m) wide **Great Wall**. Towering coconut palms swing melodically above.

On the way back to the main road, up from the historical park, stop at the 20th century **St Benedict's Church**, one of Hawaii's special places. The inside of the church is painted with biblical scenes and motifs for those who are unable to read. A bust of Father Damien, the priest who helped in the Molokai leprosy colony, stands outside.

Volcanic Action

Coffee plants and macadamia nut trees give way further south to barren black nothingness – lava flows from 1907, 1919, 1926 and 1950. Inland is the southwest rift zone of Mauna Loa, still active and potent. Forget about the cheap land for sale along the road, and instead take the turnoff for **South Point**. Many guidebooks skip over South Point, pleading a terrible road or empty desolation. Nonsense. The road is paved, although it is narrow, winding and steep, so it's necessary to be attentive to on-coming traffic. And the windswept land, like yesterday at Upolu Point, South Point is compelling and powerful. Half way down, stare at the 36 wind generators spinning like flustered mechanical flowers. Get out and listen to the *whoosh-whoosh-whoosh*. Privately owned, the **Kamoa Wind Farm** produces electricity that's sold to the public utility.

Keep bearing right to the southernmost point in the United States. Sit on the cliff edge near the Kalalea Heiau, where clear blue waters crash against the basalt cliffs. Needless to say, storms are quite impressive here. The first Polynesians to land in Hawaii probably did so here. Fishing is good off the point, attested to by the modern moorings and ladders hanging out over the 50-ft (15-m) high cliffs, and to nearby ancient canoe moorings. Due south is the Antarctic, the nearest landfall.

If the brownies weren't enough, stop in **Na`alehu**, a few more miles east on Route 11. It's a proverbially sleepy town, lovely and lined with monkeypod trees. Try **Na`alehu Coffee Shop** for fresh fish, the **Na`alehu Fruit Stand**, or the **Punalu`u Bake Shop**, justly famous for its delicious Portuguese Sweet Bread.

If you haven't already, it's time for another decision. About an hour further is **Hawaii Volcanoes National Park** (see *Itinerary 9*). If you got to an early start this morning, it's another 3 or 4 hours minimum for an extension including the park. Another possibility for a long day – and I don't recommend this at all – is to completely loop around the island through the park and Hilo, returning to Kohala and Kona from the north. Better is to spend a night in Volcano Village, if you've planned ahead for reservations, or a night in Hilo; they are 30 minutes away from each other. Both the Hawaii Volcanoes National Park and Hilo deserve more than the quick glance that continuing on now will give you.

Otherwise, backtrack along Route 11 towards Kona, taking your

Right: Pu`uhonua carving

time and maybe exploring some of those side roads that tempted you earlier, like the fishing village of **Miloli`i**, snorkeling and the Captain Cook monument at Kealakekua, or the hillside artist's town of **Holualoa**, above Kailua-Kona. Essential stops in Holualoa: **Kimura Lauhala Shop**, selling things woven from hala leaves; **Kona Art Center**, diverse in range and quality, and years ago the catalyst for Kona's development as a focus for Pacific art; some of the several galleries, especially **Studio 7**. An alternative for lodging in Kona or Kohala is the **Holualoa Inn**, a nice bed-and-breakfast.

If you're staying on in Kona or South Kohala tonight, watch the sunset from wherever impulse takes you. For local eats and atmosphere, try the pork chops at Manago's or dinner at Teshima's (see page 40). For sophisticated dining, change socks and head for the Kohala resorts: **The Canoe House** at the Mauna Lani, **The Grill** or the more formal **Dining Room** at the Orchid at Mauna Lani, or **The Batik** at the Mauna Kea. After dinner, beautiful little beaches at both hotels and lots of starlight wait patiently outside. Adding to the moon-lit magic of Mauna Kea and Kona Village are streamlined manta rays swimming in and out of the spotlights right offshore.

8: HILO *(see map, p38)*

Hawaii's biggest secret. Volcano lava flows – very fresh, very hot, and very destructive.

Hilo rates high on my list of special places, despite 120 inches (305cm) of rain annually. The rain eliminates tourist clutter, but more importantly, it makes Hilo bountiful and tropical. Exploring Hilo and surrounding areas, including Hawaii Volcanoes National Park, is time well spent. If you've added Hilo to *Itinerary 6*, eliminating Pahoa and Lava Tree State Park frees up time.

Drive to Hilo from the north, along the beautiful Hamakua coast. First impressions of Hilo often underwhelm. Hawaii's second-largest city outside Oahu, Hilo feels more like a big town, which it really is. It certainly harbors no pretenses in humoring the tourist, and thus its charm.

Like Kailua-Kona on the island's opposite side, Hilo's focus is the harbor. Tsunamis – or tidal waves – in 1946 and 1960 destroyed part of the downtown business district, but many of the old buildings remained. Pick up the brochure 'Walking Tour of Historic Downtown.' The intersection of Keawe and Waianuenue is a good reference point; a number of stores and restaurants fill the old renovated buildings. The following are good places to eat: **Bears' Coffee**, a popular hangout noted for breakfasts; **Cafe Pesto**, where the Italian fare is first rate and the prices very reasonable, which is

Left: Hilo Harbor

also true of **Pescatore's**, although the pricing's a bit higher; **Sachi's Gourmet**, which serves up cheap local Japanese-style meals; and **Cronie's**, a sports bar and restaurant which features live music Tuesday, Wednesday and Thursday evenings and draws in the locals.

A few blocks further up, the **Lyman Museum and Mission House** is a must visit. This 1839 missionary homestead has impressive 19th-century furniture. Next door, the museum's first floor is dedicated to Hawaiiana. Upstairs is the secret treasure: world-class rock-and-mineral and shell collections. In the museum's gift shop, pick up an inexpensive walking tour map of old Hilo.

Banyan Drive is Hilo's hotel district, with the very modestly priced **Hawaii Naniloa** and the **Hilo Hawaiian** both offering comfortable accommodations along with excellent coastal views. Opposite is **Lili`uokalani Gardens**, an uncrowded and serene Japanese garden of stone bridges and lions, lanterns, and a tea ceremony pavilion. Just off Banyan Drive is the **Suisan Fish Market**, where bidders compete in Japanese and heavy pidgin for the day's catch of *aku*, *mahi* and other fish from local waters. If you'd prefer accommodations with real character, book one of the five rooms at the beautifully restored **Shipman House**, built in 1899 and decorated with many of the original furnishings.

Steamy Waters

South of Hilo is a splendid scenic drive down Highway 130 towards the coast and recent lava flows. Stay on Highway 130 until the road is blocked with *pahoehoe* lava. Just beyond, scores of homes were destroyed in recent years, along with the village of **Kalapana**. Further on towards the ocean, thick steam may billow where molten lava enters the sea. Backtrack to Highway 132, then through a beautiful tunnel of trees towards **Lava Tree State Monument**, where in 1790 molten lava flooded a rainforest, then drained, leaving shells of solidified lava around now-vaporized trees. The common name for this beautiful phenomenon is a tree mold: shrouded by mists should you visit in the early morning, the place has a very eerie feel. A little further on is **Cape Kumukahi**, the island's easternmost point and site of a 1960 lava flow. Route 137 leads westward to **MacKenzie State Recreation Area**, a serene glade of ironwood trees along ocean cliffs. (As always, lock the car.)

Return to **Pahoa**, forgoing the bypass for the main town road lined with raised wooden sidewalks. Once a major supplier of *ohia* wood railroad ties to the mainland, Pahoa has an unusually high concentration of old buildings, a fact that will not be lost on you. Nothing exceptional, but fun.

Above: solidified lava blocks the road near Kalapana

9: HAWAII VOLCANOES NATIONAL PARK *(see map, p45)*

The realm of Pele, the volcano goddess. A red-hot volcano. . . Smelly vapours. . . Cool, misty heights. . . Art and artists, and a quiet place.

Although you can push for half a day, this option really deserves a full day, better yet, three or four. A compromise: stay in Hilo or in Volcano Village, and then fly out from Hilo

Start at the **Hawaii Volcanoes National Park Visitor Center** for good interpretive exhibits, and for road closure and volcanic activity information. Across the road is Volcano House, a hotel and restaurant perched on the very rim of **Kilauea Caldera**. All of the current volcanic activity is from Kilauea, which is the longest continuously erupting volcano in the world. Volcano House's location is superb, and its caldera lookout is a must; varying hues of lava on the caldera bottom betray multiple lava flows between 1885 and 1982. Recently upgraded, rooms are comfortable, though basic. The hotel dining room is to be avoided midday when tourist crowds are heavy, but offers decent fare for dinner.

Cross the road to the **Volcano Art Center**, next to the Visitor Center. Volcano is rich in creative talent, and the center's offerings are perhaps some of the best in the islands. This is the realm of Pele, the volcano goddess. Follow **Crater Rim Drive**. A few minutes past Steaming Bluff, where seeping groundwater hits hot rock, the **Hawaiian Volcano Observatory**, operated by the US Geological Survey, monitors volcanic activity. A must-visit is the **Jaggar Museum** next door.

Drive across a 1974 lava flow to the **Halema`uma`u Lookout**. The short path is sometimes veiled in smelly vapors; note the signs and health warnings. Halema`uma`u,

Top: close to the hot action
Above: heed the warning sign

a collapsed crater within Kilauea Caldera, is said to be the current abode of Pele. Believers leave gifts of *ti* leaves, coins, and flower leis on the rim.

Island to Be

Turn off onto the **Chain of Craters Road**, a road first opened in 1965 that descends down Kilauea's East Rift, which itself descends into the ocean. A new island-to-be, **Loihi**, gestates 3,000ft (915m) below the surface on the east rift and probably 100,000 years from the surface. Once it was possible to loop around to Hilo via this back way through the village of Kalapana, but Pele, ever a force to be reckoned with hereabouts, changed all that when flowing lava destroyed Kalapana. When lava flows hit the ocean, spiraling clouds of steam rise furiously hundreds of feet; twilight turns the coast into a surreal red perdition, strangely beautiful.

Returning to the Rim road, drive past the **Kilauea Iki Crater**. In 1959, a 2,000-ft (610-m) high erupting fountain issued skyward from here. The **Devastation Trail** is a somber meditation, countered by a rainforest walk to, and through, the **Thurston Lava Tube**. Other surprises demand your time: **Pua`ulu** (Bird Park); the **Tree Molds**; and my favorite, the **Mauna Iki Footprints**. As Kamehameha I was consolidating his rule over the Big Island, some fleeing warriors died on the Ka`u Desert from Kilauea's toxic gases and ash. Their footprints solidified in the ash. It's an easy trail, one of many that slice throughout the park.

Volcano Village is just minutes from the park entrance. A lot of artists have gravitated, if you can say that, to this 3,700-ft elevation (1,128-m) community. It's a quiet, reflective place. Rather than staying at the Volcano House, or even eating there, try the **Kilauea Lodge**, reservations recommended, or else the **Volcano Country Club** restaurant. (Yes, there's a golf course up here.) Several excellent bed-and-breakfast options are also in the area.

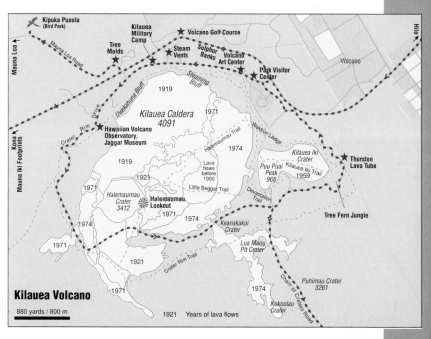

Kilauea Volcano

880 yards / 800 m

1921   Years of lava flows

Orientation

I t was not so long ago that there were no traffic lights anywhere on Kauai. While it's no longer quite that rural, Kauai remains a lush paradise, despite the occasional intrusion of shopping malls, hotels and condominiums. Kauai remains Hawaii at its most tropical and perhaps most enchanting. The northernmost of all inhabited islands in the Hawaiian chain, Kauai is rimmed by perfect, white-sand beaches that are strung like gems from Ha`ena Point on its northern coast to the ever sunny resort of Po`ipu on its southern shore, to beautiful Polihale Beach in the shadows of the Na Pali coast on its western side. However, it is also a stubborn island, both in its geographical inaccessibility and in the character of its people, as Kamehameha I learned when he tried unsuccessfully to conquer Kauai.

Testimony to the spirit and strength of Kauai is the speed with which the island bounced back after the onslaught of Hurricane Iniki in 1992. Most attractions and businesses were up and running after two years and Mother nature has quickly healed the landscape to perfection. The oldest of the inhabited islands, Kauai is probably the closest to what a tropical fantasy island *should* look like: steep green cliffs and mountainsides bedecked with cascading waterfalls seeming to fall forever; rumors of lost valleys and secretive small people called the Menehune and Mu; beaches so inaccessible and so perfect that an advertising art director couldn't do better.

Taking the Tours

Our first 2 full-day itineraries split the island in half, pivoting on the most southern point where many of the resorts and most of the sunshine is: Poipu. Lihue, the commercial and governmental hub, is ½-hour west, but with limited accommodations. Further along the eastern coast, there are a few moderately-priced hotels and resorts.

Itinerary 10 takes you along Kauai's dry leeward coast, up to the edge of Kauai's interior and an unexpected chasm in the island. *Itinerary 11* swings the other way, along the wet east coast to the north shore. Give serious thought to a night or two on the North Shore. *Itineraries 12* and *13* focus on the urban: the contemporary center of Lihue and the ancient center of Wailua. These are short options, easily done in half a day, or combined into a day. Also possible is adding the Lihue option to the end of *Itinerary 10*, and Wailua either to the start or end of *Itinerary 11*.

Right: Kilauea lighthouse
Opposite: Na Pali Coast

10: Waimea Canyon and the Leeward Coast
(see map, p50)

A breakfast sampling of fattening pastries in old sugar towns, a Russian fortress, Captain Cook's first landfall in Hawaii, the heights – and depths – of Waimea Canyon and Koke`e. End with an elegant dinner to make up for the breakfast nibbling.

As this itinerary reaches high altitudes, take a warm jacket or sweater

When the birds start twittering outside, hit the road early, not because there's a lot of driving ahead, but because you're selfish. You'd rather not share Waimea Canyon with loads of tourists. Skip a hotel breakfast: a number of places enroute encourage exploratory nibbling.

Koloa, a few minutes up the road from Poipu, is a compact place, once a sugar town but now home to an enjoyable mix of shops and restaurants that

cater to both locals and visitors. Everything will be closed right now except **Lappert's**, serving pastries, muffins and coffee. But remember, there's more up the road. From Koloa, Route 53 leads to the main island highway, Route 50. If staying in Lihue or beyond, join the itinerary here. As the road descends westward, rolling sugar cane fields climb right up to the foothills on your right. There's probably a brooding veil of clouds higher up at 5,147ft (1,600m), where the map says **Mt Wai`ale`ale** should be. I've never ever seen this remnant of Kauai's

single volcano – from either the ground or the air. That it gets a *minimum* of 450 inches (1,143cm) of rain annually could explain its fleetingness. But no worries. Hawaiian weather can be extremely local; less than 10 miles (16km) from Wai`ale`ale – the world's rainiest place – it hardly rains at all.

Drive past Ele`ele and Port Allen. A couple of blinks beyond, watch for **Hanapepe** and head into town. Like most sugar towns now, Hanapepe looks passed up by the future. But there's a renewed spark simmering in town. The road passes several galleries in old storefronts, worth a look on the return. For now, continue breakfast: pastries and espresso at **Hanapepe Cafe & Espresso** in town, or a Kauai-style omelet with Portuguese sausage at the **Green Garden Restaurant**, near the highway.

Outside Hanapepe, down by the ocean, are ancient salt ponds, but there's not much to see. Continue to Waimea. Just before town, the ruins of **Fort Elizabeth** recall a fascinating, but mostly insignificant episode in Hawaii's history. In 1815, a Russian ship was shipwrecked near Waimea, and Kauai's king claimed its cargo. An agent of the czar was sent to negotiate return of the valuable cargo. He got carried away and tried to negotiate for a slice of Hawaii as well. The fort begun in 1816 as part of the deal, but the deal collapsed – the czar

Above: Fort Elizabeth
Right: Statue of Captain Cook

kauai

preferred Alaska instead. Climb the fort's red rock walls to take in Waimea Bay, where Captain Cook made his first Hawaiian landfall in 1778; an unassuming statue of Cook acknowledges this seminal event.

In **Waimea**, turn inland for Waimea Canyon Road. But first, stop at **Yumi's**. The window says, 'sushi and pies,' but inside heavenly cinnamon rolls await. Now, onward. Waimea Canyon Road lumbers upward, eventually yielding to rousing views of Waimea Canyon. There are several lookouts where you can watch mists, rainbows, shadows and colors shift like atmospheric alchemy in this 3,500-ft (1,060-m) deep, 10-mile (16-km) long chasm.

Continue on past the second canyon lookout to **Koke`e State Park**, with its impressive trails and spectacular views from lookouts along the 4,000-ft (1,200-m) rim of **Kalalau Valley**. But the view of Kalalau is quite temperamental and whimsical; it may be there or not, obscured by clouds and mists below. If so, wait a few minutes or return later, or at last resort, buy a postcard. If not visible, here's what you're missing: the swooping valley drops 4,000-ft (1,200-m) down to a beautiful beach, the terminus of an 11-mile (17-km) hiking trail originating at the other end of the Na Pali Coast, near Hanalei. The valley is ennobled by steep, graceful, and vibrantly-green cliff walls.

Birds and Sacred Ruins

Swing back to Koke'e State Park, an important refuge for many of Hawaii's indigenous – and endangered – birds. **Koke'e Lodge** has a dozen economical and rustic cabins, and a decent finish to your breakfast survey, if still hungry, is at the restaurant nearby. Nothing elegant, but satisfying in this high, cool air. Stop at the museum for a brief on the area's natural history, and for walking and hiking information.

Follow the road back down to the coast, keeping right at the fork midway. At the bottom drive through the tidy neighborhoods of **Kekaha**, past the hissing sugar mill and onto Route 50. You could backtrack towards Waimea, but why not continue to road's end? **Polihale State Park** will surprise you with a big and moody beach and even bigger and moodier cliffs. Follow the signs. Forget about swimming at Polihale, but do contemplate the waves, and the cliffs to the north, the start of the awesome Na Pali Coast. Nearby are the ruins of the **Polihale Heiau**, difficult to find. This is a sacred place where spirits of the dead leap into the afterlife.

Return to Waimea past sunny, scenic, and almost always nearly-empty beaches. Tempted? Plenty of time, although it's better to avoid

Right: Waimea Canyon views

the unpredictable currents and enjoy beachcombing rather than swimming. Curious about that flat-top island across the way? It's **Niʻihau**, inhabited, Hawaiian-speaking, and no tourists allowed, thank you, although several companies do make summer trips to Niʻihau's coastal waters on dive tours. Also of interest in Waimea are the **ancient salt pans**, in use since Polynesian times for evapo-

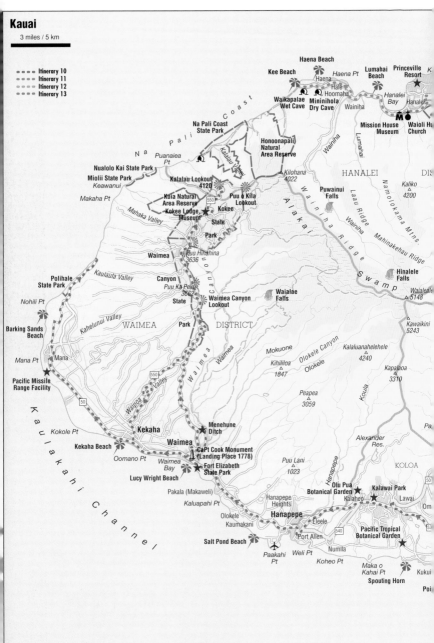

Kauai

3 miles / 5 km

- - - - Itinerary 10
- - - - Itinerary 11
- - - - Itinerary 12
- - - - Itinerary 13

k a u a i

rating ocean water to create sea salt. Follow Ala Wai Road, which parallels Waimea Stream, to reach the **Menehune Ditch**, a Polynesian-era irrigation channel said to have been built by Kauai's legendary menehune. Go over the nearby hanging bridge that crosses Waimea Stream for lovely rural views that include taro patches that supply the raw material for the nearby **Makaweli Poi Factory**, on Waimea Road, which always provides a warm welcome to visitors. If early morning views up topside were hidden, consider a return to Waimea and Koke'e.

Stay on Route 50 to Route 530, which funnels you back to Koloa via an impressive tunnel of eucalyptus trees. Or consider continuing to Lihue (see *Itinerary 12*).

As the Sun Sets

In Koloa, you can scout the shops along the old wooden sidewalk. Across from the main shopping area is a stone chimney – it is all that's left of Kauai's first sugar mill built in 1835, and a monument to sugar's heyday.

If it's approaching sunset, it is perhaps time to sit. The Poipu beach area is perfect, either from the sand or at **Brennecke's Beach Broiler** along Hoone Road. For an elegant evening, try **Roy's Poipu Bar & Grill** in the Poipu Shopping Village, or **Tidepools** at the Hyatt Regency Kauai. If it's drinks you're in the mood for, head to **Stevenson's** (as in Robert Louis) also at the Hyatt Regency. A short drive away in Puhi, off Route 50, is **Gaylord's**, a restaurant in a beautifully restored 1930s plantation-era mansion where al fresco dining includes lovely mountain views.

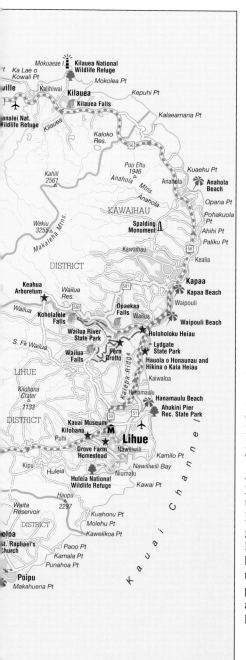

11: HANALEI AND THE NORTH SHORE *(see map, p50)*

Maybe the most beautiful place on earth. Along the way: ancient sites, a lighthouse and birds with 8-ft (2½-m) wingspans, a prince of a golf resort, an old bridge with omnipotent powers.

If possible, consider spending a night, or several. Take an umbrella

Today you can't get on the road early enough, simply because one of the most stunning places anywhere waits on the North Shore: Hanalei and the road's end. From Poipu, find Highway 50 and drive east towards Lihue. Depending on the time, a morning rush hour of sorts may be going into Lihue; although perhaps a surprise, it doesn't last long. Continue on to Wailua, both covered in *Itineraries 12* and *13*. It's possible to do part or all of the Wailua portion here, for example, **Poli`ahu Heiau** and **Opaeka`a Falls**.

A few minutes beyond Wailua is **Kapa`a**, a humming and popping town with no touristy sights except restaurants and stores. Stop by **Michelle's Cafe & Bakery** for breakfast and pastries. For something heftier and traditional, the **Ono Family Restaurant** is popular. In the Hee Fat Marketplace, note **The Big Wave Brewing Company**, one of three microbreweries on the island, for a later lunch. Recommended for dinner on the return is the Hawaiian regional cuisine at **A Pacific Cafe**.

Kilauea Views and Wildlife

The road eases around the northeast edge of Kauai to the North Shore. A must-visit: **Kilauea National Wildlife Refuge**, not for the 1913 lighthouse – said to have the world's largest (12-ft/3½-m high) clamshell lens – but rather

for the gorgeous views of the coast and wondrous seabirds riding the wind. Watch out especially for the frigate bird, hard to ignore with its 8-ft (2½-m) wingspan. Odds are uncertain, but scan the ocean 700ft (210m) below for turtles, whales, dolphins, and the rare Hawaiian monk seal. Bad eyes? Borrow a pair of binoculars at the visitors center, where you can also sign up for a naturalist-led tour.

Coming or going to the lighthouse, stop in Kilauea town at the **Kong Lung Store**, housed in an 1881 plantation store. A tomato's throw away is **Casa di Amici**, with relaxing ambiance and excellent pasta – and a good wine list, too. Lighter fare, including incredible smoothies, are to be had at **Mango Mama's** and **Banana Joe's**, both just off the main highway.

Left: Hanalei Bay

kauai

Past Kilauea, the highway passes through gentle countryside with views of the island's mountainous interior. You'll pass the small **Princeville Airport** where Hawaiian Helicopters departs on spectacular aerial tours. The road starts to narrow, anticipating an even narrower road later on.

You can't miss it: the 1,000-acre (400-ha) **Princeville Resort**, named after Kamehameha IV's son, Prince Albert. Blessed with exceptional scenery,

even by Hawaii standards, the resort has 45-holes of scenic, world-class golf, a shopping center and single family houses and condos. Drive through the resort to the **Princeville Hotel**, one of Hawaii's nicest luxury hotels. The decor is Euro-elegant, with plenty of marble and antiques. But it is quickly apparent that the setting is the hotel's best asset, revealed by floor-to-ceiling windows that take in a view of steep-walled mountains draped in waterfalls, and Hanalei Bay. Hanalei Bay is a favorite spot of yachtsmen in summer, giving way to surfers in winter when the big waves from the north roll in. The Princeville's **Cafe Hanalei** serves up both the view and excellent meals. If you are in Hanalei tonight, reserve a window table at **La Cascata** Italian restaurant.

On the main highway beyond the Princeville entrance is a lookout of **Hanalei Valley**, which provides half of Hawaii's poi from the cultivated taro fields below. The wetlands offer refuge for birds; the lower extent of Hanalei Valley is a national wildlife refuge. The road twists down to the Hanalei River. A 1913 vintage one-lane bridge, cherished by local residents because it effectively slows things to suit the rural setting, carries you across.

New-Age Hangout

Hanalei is home to an interesting community, a lifestyle stew of true *kama`aina*, surfers, New Age types, bankers and celebrities in hiding, and more than its fair share of beach bums. The main commercial center is **Ching Young Village**, good for bee pollen, *The New York Times*, T-shirts or camping gear. The **Hanalei Gourmet** offers eclectic fare with an Hawaiian regional twist, a casual atmosphere, and live music on select nights. The **Hanalei Dolphin** takes advantage of its streamside setting that makes al fresco dining an option, with fresh fish the specialty. Check out **Sushi Blues** if sushi's your preference.

Down the road on the left is a New England-looking green church. This is the **Wai`oli Hui`ia Church**, more easily pronounced 'the green church.' Visit the **Wai`oli Mission House Museum** (tel: 245 3202; Tuesday, Thursday, Saturday, 9am–3pm) behind it.

Above: taro worker
Right: cattle egret

The road from Hanalei to the end of civilization is distinctly rural as it winds through picturesque streams and one-lane bridges, passing beautiful empty beaches and simple houses on million-dollar plots of land. At the far end of Hanalei Bay, opposite the Princeville Hotel, the road begins to twist and shoot past **Lumaha`i Beach**, made famous in *South Pacific*. A truly beautiful beach, it is flanked by black lava rock. Despite its daytime popularity, I've experienced dozens of dusks from the beach with not another soul in sight. The **Hanalei Colony Resort** further along has condo-style accommodations, simple in personality but on the beach. A family with children couldn't do better.

As the Sun Sets
Around **Ha`ena Beach** are several caves along the road. Called **wet or dry** caves for obvious reasons, they are actually ancient lava tubes, some extending a mile back. Another couple of minutes further is the end of the road and **Ke`e Beach**. Midday is crowded here, as are weekends. In summer, the snorkeling's quite good, but winter turns the waves into monsters. The trailhead for the Kalalau Trail (Remember yesterday's lookout?) starts here: Eleven miles (18km) of gorgeous but strenuous trail snake along the Na Pali coastline, skirting isolated beaches and ocean caves. The first 2 miles (1 mile up, 1 mile down) make a great day trip that includes coastal panoramas and takes you to pristine **Hanakapiai Valley**. You can head to the coast, where a wide beach exists during the summer (in winter it's washed away by high surf). Do not swim here as the currents are dangerous, even when waters look calm and inviting. You can also head inland on a 2-mile-long loop trail that leads to towering **Hanakapiai Falls**. Near the trailhead is the **Lohiau Hula Platform**, dedicated to the goddess of hula.

Despite lots of people during the day, sunsets usually blossom on a nearly-empty Ke`e Beach, a good reason for staying late or all night in Hanalei.

12: LIHUE *(see map, p50)*

An easy ½ day with two estate homes to visit, Menehune handiwork, an upstream kayak excursion, and, yes, a museum. Kitschy Hawaiiana and noodles too.

Kauai's recent history is virtually synonymous with the Wilcox name, one of the early missionary families. **Kilohana**, on Route 50 between Poipu and Lihue, is one of several grand old **Wilcox estates**. Several of the rooms of this 1930s Tudor-style mansion have been restored, providing a sense of luxury as it was once lived on Kauai. Others now house galleries and boutiques. Around a courtyard outside is **Gaylord's**, one of the island's best restaurants. If time permits, you can also take a horse-drawn carriage ride around the estate grounds.

Like nearly every other town on Kauai, Lihue started with sugar. It's now Kauai's largest community and its governmental seat. It's not a tourist locus, but there are a couple of things to see. Begin at the **Kauai Museum**, on Rice Street. Once the public library, the museum packs a lot of natural history and people history into an hour or two. It often offers ½-day courses in such activities as *lau hala* weaving and lei-making. A gallery upstairs displays the work of local artists, and excellent books and maps may be found in its gift shop. Open on weekdays and Saturday mornings.

Plantation Home

Located on Nawiliwili Road, on the outskirts of Lihue, the **Grove Farm Homestead** is the former home of George N, another member of the Wilcox clan who was hands-on founder of the Grove Farm sugar plantation. Older than Kilohana (the earliest portions of the house date to the mid-800s), it is far more of a working homestead than the estate of the landed gentry. With original furnishings throughout, the escorted tour offers a unique glimpse of plantation lifestyle. Offered twice daily on Monday, Wednesday and Thursday, the 2-hour-long tours are limited to 12 participants. Reservations are a must. As tours are usually a sell-out, advance bookings (up to 3 months in advance) are recommended.

Continue down Rice Street towards Nawiliwili, Kauai's picturesque but commercial harbor. At the pier where the inter-island cruise ships dock, bear right past a huge, monolithic gray warehouse – stored sugar cane for shipment to the mainland – to Hulemalu Road.

The road climbs to a lookout on the left. Below you is the **Alakoko Fishpond**, fed by the Hule`ia Stream descending from the Hoary Head Mountains beyond. Sometimes called the **Menehune Fishpond**, legend says the Menehune – little leprechaun-like people gifted with amazing building skills

Above: Kauai Museum
Opposite above: happy hikers; **opposite left:** and a reason to stay out late

and here long before the Polynesians arrived – built the pond. An ancient example of aqua-farming, this pond is part of the **Hule`ia National Wildlife Refuge**, home to endangered waterfowl species. For a more intimate view of the setting, join an escorted kayak excursion upstream to the headwaters (see *Activities* chapter).

Return to Nawiliwili and head for the Kauai Lagoons resort, home of the Kauai Marriott. This was formerly the Westin Kauai but took a major hit from Hurricane Iniki in 1992 and was remodeled and reopened as the Kauai Marriott, with Hawaiian-style gardens replacing the previous European-style water fountains and horse-drawn coaches with frilly trim. The Whaler's Brew Pub, a beachfront microbrewery provides a great place for sunset, while Duke's Canoe Club, one of Kauai's favorite hangouts, offers seafood, with surfing memorabilia that creates an appealing sense of place. A cheaper alternative is back in town, at **Hamura Saimin**, on Kress Street, serving great finest noodle soup, Hawaiian-style.

13: WAILUA *(see map, p50)*

Investigations of the royal places along the Wailua River.

Highway 56 leads from Lihue towards **Wailua**, about 10 miles (16km) up the road. Around where the **Wailua River** meets the ocean are a large number of ancient Hawaiian sites. The royal Hawaiians held this area as sacred, and thus *kapu* to commoners. You could poke around for hours, preferably in the early morning or late afternoon.

Kauai legends and oral traditions are among Hawaii's richest. In the last

decade, visible remnants that embody ancient Hawaiian culture have become popular with travelers, including a gathering of rocks at Wailua, a few hundred yards up Kuamo`o Road towards the mountains from the Coco Palms Hotel. Two stones, a birthstone and a *piko* (navel) stone, make this a sacred place. Women of high rank bore their children at the birthstone to ensure their babies would be chiefs, then disposed of the umbilical cords at the *piko* stone.

Before crossing the Wailua River bridge, turn right for **Lydgate State Park**, a favorite local beach with full facilities and a nice, protected swimming area. Walk towards the river. A grove of coconut palms shelters the **Hauola o Honaunau**, a place of refuge for fugitives

Above: hanging out at Duke's; **left:** Opaeka`a Falls; **opposite:** making a splash

in old Hawaii, and the **Hikina o Kala Heiau**. Take care as these sites remain sacred for many Hawaiians.

Just after the bridge, turn left onto Highway 580. Two miles (3km) up on the right is a parking lot for **Opaeka`a Falls**, most spectacular after heavy rains on Mt Wai`ale`ale. You can't see them, but shrimp lay eggs in the pool at the bottom of the 40-ft (12-m) waterfall. Walk across the road for a broad view of the Wailua River gently snaking below, once lined with secret sacred temples all the way up to its origin on Wai`ale`ale; cliffs and bluffs along the way were *ali`i* burial places.

On the river, barge-like boats carry paying tourists to **Fern Grotto**, where ferns grow profusely at the mouth of a lava tube. It's commercially promoted ad nauseam as a must-see but is actually quite ignorable because of the intrusive showbiz style of the tour operator, both on the river and at the grotto. Better to spend your time and money visiting the streamside Kamakila Hawaiian Cultural Village or renting a kayak and paddling up the river at your own pace. No forced serenades, no elbow-to-elbow crowds, just the beauty that is Kauai. Bring a picnic, take your time.

Sacrificial Shrines

Back on Highway 580, close to the main highway, there are several sacred outdoor shrines, including the **Poli`ahu Heiau**. Nearby is a bell stone, which rang out when hit with a stone to announce royal births. **Holoholoku Heiau**, a sacrificial altar with royal birthstones nearby, is an older heiau, and has more than coincidental resemblance to Tahitian temples. The rest of the day, get into the local pace of life. If you want to pick up some postcards, bypass the sprawling tourist-oriented Coconut Marketplace, instead, drop by the local supermarket or drugstore. Take in one of the weekly county-sponsored **Sunshine Markets**, where the fresh produce and flowers are in abundance.

Grab some Portuguese bean soup and pie at **Ono Family Restaurant** on Highway 56. If evening approaches, catch sunset from the beach. For dinner, head back to **A Pacific Cafe** in Kapa`a or stop at **Gaylord's** on the way back to Poipu. If you're ready for some laughs, check out the weekly **Comedy Club** at the Kauai Marriott Beach Club and Villas, close to Lihue.

Orientation

Nobody traveling to Hawaii ever says they're going to Oahu, the Big Island, or Kauai. But they can say *I'm going to Maui*. Indeed, Maui's recognition quotient – not to mention its array of shopping and cuisine – is exceeded in Hawaii only by Oahu's Waikiki.

Maui is just the tip of a tropical iceberg, so to speak. The second largest of Hawaii's 130-plus islands and the only island namesake of a god, Maui is the exposed top of a 30,000-ft (9,144-m) high mountain. Two volcanoes formed Maui: the older and eroded West Maui volcano, and Haleakala, topping out at 10,023ft (3,055m), although when Maui was an adolescent, it was nearly 14,000ft (4,200m), higher even than the Big Island today.

The largest dormant volcano on earth, Haleakala necessarily defines Maui's size and character. Its rainshadow yields two superb and sunny beach areas, Ka`anapali in West Maui, and Wailea/Kihei in South Maui. Haleakala's gentle slopes nurture a winery, world-class artists, some of the best onions anywhere, some weird but fascinating flowers, and one of the few remaining preserves of indigenous Hawaiian flora and fauna.

Taking the Tours

The full-day tours (see *Itinerary 14* and *15)* favor time flexibility. If you're demonically possessed, a few hours will do. If slothfully disposed, the itineraries can last from dawn to dusk. *Itinerary 14* hugs the West Maui Mountains, with Lahaina or Ka`anapali as start and finish. It's a good day for roaming, browsing and shopping; a prodigious number of restaurants baits us relentlessly. *Itinerary 15* has loftier ambitions: to climb to the very summit of Haleakala. Later, you'll wander across Haleakala's lower slopes, known as Upcountry.

The Hana Highway, and Molokai and Lanai (see *Itineraries 16* and *17*) are full-day tours at minimum, but highly recommended nonetheless. The first is a meandering drive to the very eastern edge of the island, where one of the island's most bucolic towns awaits: Hana. Hawaiians say that 'the sky comes close to Hana,' and, indeed, moody clouds often hang low off the hills here. *Itinerary 17* includes the islands of Molokai and Lanai. Together with uninhabited Kaho`olawe, this row of sheltering islands forms one side of the Au`au Channel, which protects Maui's dry shores and creates a haven for humpback whales in winter. While certainly less cosmopolitan than internationally-famous Maui, Molokai and Lanai are both equally fascinating and add to the diversity of the County of Maui. Each island is worthy of day trips from Maui. But better yet, budget more time so that you can spend a night or two soaking up the attractions on each one.

NENE CROSSING NEXT 2 MI.

Right: watch out for the endangered nene
Opposite: Haleakala Crater, by horse

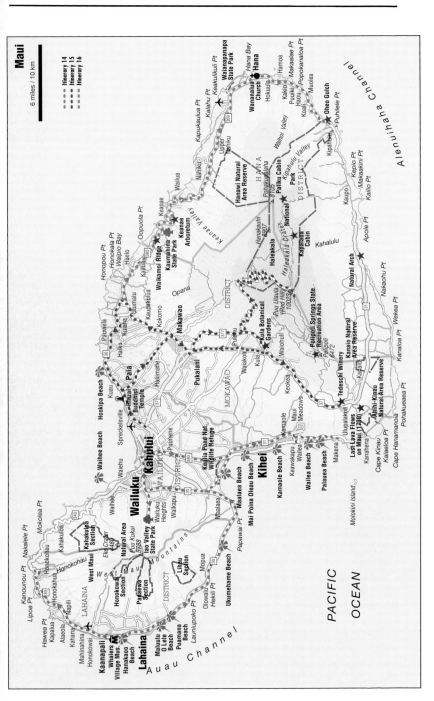

14: WEST MAUI AND LAHAINA *(see map, p60)*

An easy day in West Maui: `Iao Valley State Park, Wailuku, hotels and shopping and eating in Ka`anapali and Kapalua. Maybe a side trip to South Maui. Sunset and dinner in Lahaina.

This itinerary centers on West Maui, starting and finishing in Lahaina or Ka`anapali. If staying in South Maui, you'll intercept the itinerary between Lahaina and Wailuku

You can't help but notice the **West Maui Mountains**, an eroded and extinct volcano, now lusciously green and often embroidered with rainbows. A valley – once the volcano's crater – is your first stop. Only Route 30 heads south out of Lahaina: take it, passing beach parks with clear views across the Au`au Channel of **Molokai**, **Lanai**, and **Kaho`olawe**, all part of Maui County. Between November and April, humpback whales nurture newborn-young in the sheltered waters. In season, stop and watch.

The road bends inland across lowlands connecting West Maui with **Haleakala**, the conspicuous and dormant volcano to the right. Signs point to Wailuku, Maui's government seat and an old sugar town nestled in the foothills above the more commercial Kahului. Continue on through both Kahului and Wailuku; you'll stop in Wailuku later.

Water, Water Everywhere

`Iao Valley State Park – the volcano's ancient crater at road's end – is idyllic, verdantly green, and indubitably wet – 408 inches (1,036cm) of rainfalls yearly on the 5,788-ft (1,764-m) high Pu`u Kukui nearby; Lahaina, just 8 miles (13km) away by air, gets 20 inches (50cm). A stream skirts `Iao Needle, the valley's 1,200-ft (366-m) high focus, then descends to Wailuku, which means 'water of destruction' – a bloody battle was fought here during Kamehameha's 1790 Maui conquest.

Returning to **Wailuku**, turn left onto Market Street, then to Vineyard Street. This business neighborhood is undergoing modest renovation and is good for a reconnoiter. Several so-called antique shops are clustered here, filled mostly with dusty but wonderful old things and some tantalizing Hawaiiana memorabilia. Wailuku also has some interesting crafts shops. Stop by the **Maui Rehabilitation Center** on Mahalani Street, which has good prices on locally-made works. Two casual but quality Thai restaurants – **Siam Thai** on Market and **Saeng's Thai Cuisine** on Vineyard – lure travelers and locals alike. For local atmosphere, **Sam Sato's**, further along down Market Street, is perfect for noodles and manju. Have

Right: idyllic `Iao Valley

a hankering for a museum? **Hale Ho`ike`ike** – the Bailey Missionary House – is a good museum of both traditional Hawaiian and missionary life.

Leaving Wailuku, dash through Kahului, which has little of interest except essential shopping. But do consider a side trip to **South Maui**, especially Wailea and Makena, with beaches and sunshine as good as, if not better, than Ka`anapali. Bypass Kihei, an uninspired strip of condos and shopping centers. **Wailea**, however, is a luxury resort with deluxe hotels and condos that include the extravagant **Grand Wailea**, the elegant **Four Seasons**, the tasteful **Renaissance Wailea Beach**, and the all-suites **Kea Lani**. For some sly humor, look at the **Fernando Botero sculptures** at the **Grand Wailea Resort**.

Follow Routes 31 and 30 back to West Maui. Save Lahaina for last, so you'll bypass both it and Ka`anapali on your way north to the **Kapalua Resort**, a low-profile development that blends in with an exquisite setting and a world-class infrastructure to offer Hawaii at its best. Besides superb golf (three courses), tennis (two 10-court complexes), beaches and a deluxe mix of hotels and condominiums, the food is worthy of mention. Try the oceanside **Bay Club**, the **Plantation Restaurant** at the Plantation Golf Course clubhouse, or **Sansei** at the Kapalua Shops, for superb Japanese fare.

Return towards Ka`anapali, or continue to **Honokohau** (not to be confused with Honokahua, which is closer to Ka`anapali), a village on the coast amidst rugged views and pristine quiet.

Ka`anapali** was developed as Hawaii's first planned resort nearly 40 years ago. Although over-developed for those seeking a quiet getaway, **Ka`anapali still draws some of Hawaii's highest occupancies thanks to a mix of quality hotels and condominiums, and facilities that include two golf courses, tennis, 2-mile long stretches of beach, shops and restaurants, and a promenade that offers plenty of people-watching.

Above: fossilized salt
Opposite: Front Street

Whales

Visit Hawaii in winter and you'll have company: about 600 humpback whales down from Alaskan waters. Here to mate, give birth, and nurture newborn, whales like privacy – federal law requires a 300-ft (100-m) distance for whale watchers. This is strictly enforced by arrest and fine, and occasionally jail, as more than one ignorant tourist has learned.

Having said that, definitely go whale-watching. You can see whales anywhere, even off Diamond Head, but your safest bet is in the sheltered waters between Maui, Molokai, Lanai, and Kaho`olawe. Don't worry about finding a whale-watching boat on Maui. They'll find you. I prefer the Pacific Whale Foundation's or Captain Nemo's excursions, not exactly luxurious like the big boats, but sure adventure.

• *Whale watching season*: November through April, best January through March.

• *How to know you've seen a whale*: when they spout – inhaling and exhaling on the surface – and when they fluke, spy hop, and breach.

• *Number of whales in Hawaii*: About 600, a mere fraction of a century ago.

• *Data*: 10–15ft (3½–4½m) long at birth, weighing 1–3 tons (1,016–3,048kg). Newborns gain 200 lbs (90½kg) a day. Adults average 40 tons (40,642kg) in weight..

South Beach is the more crowded of the beaches, providing a setting for the **Regency Maui**, the **Maui Marriott**, the **Westin Maui**, the **Ka`anapali Beach Resort** and the **Sheraton Maui** as well as the **Whaler** and **Ka`anapali Ali`i** condominiums. **North Beach** is far less crowded with only the **Royal Lahaina** on the beach. Even if you're not staying at Ka`anapali, don't miss the **Whalers Village**, which has a good selection of restaurants and two first-rate museums, one on whales, the other on whaling.

Whaling Capital

Speaking of whaling... South of Ka`anapali, take the first turnoff for **Lahaina**, the Pacific's whaling capital in the early 1800s. It's hard to get lost in Lahaina. Its main street is **Front Street**, paralleling the waterfront. The **Pioneer Inn** and nearby banyan tree are good navigation references. The banyan tree is *the* **Banyan Tree**, planted in 1873 and now extending its canopy nearly an acre. The Pioneer Inn, built in 1901 for inter-island ferry passengers, has not-so-quiet rooms that are plain but economical.

Don't ignore Lahaina's side streets. Take a look at two cozy and elegant hotels down Lahainaluna Road. The **Lahaina Hotel**, packed with collectible antiques, has waterfront views. Further down is the **Plantation Inn**. Both are delightful resort alternatives, each with a fine restaurant. Available almost everywhere is a brochure outlining a historical walking tour. Two suggested stops are the **Wo Hing Temple**, built by a Chinese fraternal society in 1912 and now showing old Thomas Edison films of Hawaii, and the **Baldwin House**, across from the Pioneer Inn. At the top end of Front Street is the **Lahaina Jodo Mission**, where the largest Buddha outside of Asia ponders sunsets and yet more sunsets.

In Lahaina, what's new is in equal abundance to what's old. **Planet Hollywood** restaurant presides on Front Street. The **Hard Rock Cafe** is equally popular. If sunset approaches, drop anchor. Lahaina is one of the few places in Hawaii with several pubs and restaurants right on the water – **Kimo's** for seafood; **Cheeseburger in Paradise** for the obvious; **Lahaina Fish Co** because they catch their own... The list could continue.

Lahaina stays open late by Maui standards, and the night is limited only by your stamina and tomorrow's schedule. It's your vacation, after all.

15: HALEAKALA AND UPCOUNTRY *(see maps, p60 & p64)*

The summit of Haleakala. A winery and strange flowers. Windsurfers and cowboys.

Bring warm clothes; there's a 30-degree difference between the beach and Haleakala's summit, usually amplified by a wind chill factor

It's to be a wondrous day atop **Haleakala**, a dormant – meaning definitely not extinct – volcano. Haleakala roughly translates as 'house used by the sun,' appropriate for the summit sunrises and sunsets. Depending on what you did or didn't do last night, you might consider watching the Pacific's finest sunrise from atop Haleakala (10,023ft/3,040m). Note the qualifier, *might*. A summit sunrise requires a three-in-the-morning wake-up call. If you pass on sunrise, you'll need an early start anyway – by seven at the latest – as the summit often vanishes beneath clouds by late morning.

Start near Kahului airport on Route 36. There's a turnoff for the Haleakala Highway (Route 37) but *don't take it* unless you're chasing a summit sunrise. Instead, continue past the airport along Route 36 a few more miles to **Lower Pa`ia**, an old sugar town taken over by windsurfers and their entourages. (Route 36 continues to Hana, see *Itinerary 16*.) Turn off and continue up towards Pa`ia – for breakfast, try **Charley's**. Further along is **Makawao**, a serious *paniolo*

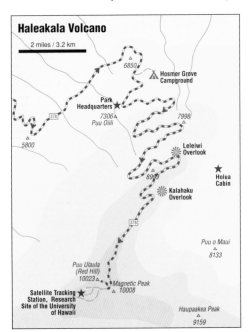

Haleakala Volcano

2 miles / 3.2 km

△ 6850

⚡ Hosmer Grove Campground

Park Headquarters ★
7306 △
Puu Oiili

△ 7998

378

△ 5800

⚡ Leleiwi Overlook

△ 8999

★ Holua Cabin

⚡ Kalahaku Overlook

378

Puu o Maui
△ 8133

Puu Ulaula
(Red Hill)
10023 △
Magnetic Peak
△ 10008

Satellite Tracking ★
Station, Research
Site of the University
of Hawaii

Haupaakea Peak
△ 9159

Above: Haleakala Crater

maui

town settled by Portuguese immigrants working on area ranches. Its rough edges are softening with a scattering of new galleries, shops, and eateries.

Follow the signs for Haleakala. You're 'upcountry' now, on Haleakala's gentle slopes where the air is often brisk and the mood content. The final stretch of road, after zigzagging through Makawao and Pukalani, twists like a crazed serpent all the way to Haleakala's top, taking about an hour. The road could be slick, even icy, and sometimes wrapped in fog. **Haleakala National Park** is the prize at road's end. The park encompasses the 19-sq mile (49-sq km), 3,000-ft (915-m) deep **Haleakala Crater**, plus Haleakala's eastern slope to the ocean. The crater view is simply breathtaking – further adjectives fail miserably and I won't try. On the opposite side 7 miles (11½km) away is **Kipahulu Valley**, a nature preserve and rainforest closed to the public; the valley drops down Haleakala's east slope. Contemplate the crater from two lookouts: **Kalahaku** and **Pu`u Ula`ula**, at the summit. Feel the crater itself by hiking along some of its many miles of trails for an hour or for several days. Or take a horse down. Near the Pu`u Ula`ula summit lookout is a satellite tracking station tended by the federal government and the University of Hawaii. Don't try getting in, because it's closed to the public.

Barren Bloom

Although seemingly barren, Haleakala is refuge for two unique species: the remarkable silversword plant with their dagger-shaped silvery leaves and the nene goose. Related to the sunflower, silversword plants – Hawaii's official state flower and unique to the Hawaiian islands – sometimes wait two decades or so before blooming just once before dying. Growing up to a height of 3–8ft (1–2½m), silverswords most commonly burst forth their flowers from June through October. The nene goose, once nearly extinct, lacks the webbed feet so essential for negotiating the craggy lava rock.

Powerful as Haleakala is on the mind and spirit, eventually you've got to come down along the same road. At the bottom, turn left onto Route 377 towards **Kula**. The climate here is nearly perfect for the beautiful protea flower – you might stop at one of several protea farms in the Kula area. The **Kula Lodge** is good for a late breakfast or for dinner if you wait at the summit for the sunset. Follow Route 37 south as it narrows over idyllic countryside, more like Ireland or Kentucky than tropical Hawaii. Alalakeiki Channel lies ahead; you can see Kahoolawe, Lanai, Molokai, and a cute half moon islet called Molokini, popular snorkeling spot. Long ago, during one of the ice ages when sea levels were 300ft (90m) lower, all these islands and Maui were one big island. Along South Maui's coast, the resorts of Wailea look rather tiny from this 3,000-ft (900-m) elevation. To the far left of Wailea, past Makena, is Maui's most recent lava flow, c. 1790.

Just past the rustic general store of Ulupalakua Ranch is the **Tedeschi Winery**, once the site of a sugar mill and since 1974 the only commercial

Above: the strangely beautiful protea flower

winery in Hawaii, producing unique island brews like pineapple wine and Ulupalakua Red. Wine connoisseurs might raise their eyebrows, but I suggest you get a bottle or two for a sunset picnic on the beach later. After a few minutes in the tasting room, a retired 100-year-old jail, tour the winery and stretch your legs before heading back towards Kula.

Stay left on Route 37 towards Pukalani. In Pukalani, turn right to Makawao for an hour or two of browsing or eating. Try **Polli's** for Mexican food, or **Casanova Italian Restaurant**, which has a good takeout deli. Rather than take the main road to Pa`ia, continue down to the coast on Route 400, a nice backcountry road. At the junction, left is Route 36, right is 360 – the Hana Highway. *Don't even think about a quick jaunt to Hana right now*, not unless you're spending the night in Hana. (See *Itinerary 16*.) Turn left and follow Route 36 along the coast towards Kahului. A few minutes before Pa`ia, stop at **Ho`okipa Beach**, either at a lookout on one of the bluffs, or at the beach parking lot. Ho`okipa is a world-class windsurfing spot because of ideal waves and wind. On good days – for the diehard, that means every day – scores of windsurfers, many of them competitive professionals, ride the waves and wind.

Dinner options: **Mama's Fish House** near Ho`okipa Beach, pasta and live music at **Casanova's**, or uncork that wine over a picnic by the beach. A return to Haleakala's summit for sunset is not that crazy of an idea, either.

16: HANA HIGHWAY *(see map, p60)*

A day trip along the famous Hana Highway to the town of Hana and Ohe`o Gulch with its refreshing pools.

Forget the silly T-shirts trumpeting 'survival' of the **Hana Highway**. It's nonsense; locals commute on the highway everyday. Built by convicts over half a century ago, the Hana Highway is a fine road, narrow but paved and well-marked. There are, however, some tight curves that make for slow travel. Over 600 curves, by some counts, so drive carefully.

The road requires a full day round trip at minimum, and a full tank of gas. If this is to be a day trip, then leave early. By late morning, traffic peaks.

Returning, traffic is heavy in late afternoon. Plan on 3–4 hours, one way. You might do better, but enjoy yourself, for the road itself is the main attraction.

The Hana Highway takes off on its own where the road changes from Route 36 to 360, at the junction with Route 400 beyond Ho`okipa Beach. In Pa`ia, top off the gas tank and pick up a picnic lunch at **Picnics**; breakfasts are good here, too.

The highway's scenery is predictable: rich and lush forests, resplendent waterfalls at nearly every bend (or so it seems) and fine ocean vistas. Pleasant rest stops, now or on the return: **Waikamoi Ridge Trail Nature Walk**, **Kaumahina State Park**, and **Ke`anae Arboretum**. There's a dandy lookout above the small Hawaiian community of **Wailua**, nestled amidst cultivated taro. A must-stop, just before Hana, is **Wai`anapanapa State Park**, with its black-sand beach and caves.

Pool, Falls and Hana

Hana itself is nearly anticlimactic after the drive. Rippling with quiet and unruffled serenity, there's hardly a touristy touch anywhere, save the tourists themselves. The cross which commands the slopes above Hana honors Paul Fagan, who built the hotel and started the ranch in the 1940s. Accommodations run the gamut. The **Hotel Hana-Maui** is an expensive, low-profile retreat favored by those who want privacy or just a fine meal. Other equally idyllic if more rustic accommodations include the **Aloha Cottages** on a bed and breakfast. House rentals and a few cute bed and breakfasts are also on hand, or you can stay in one of the rustic state cabins at Wai`anapanapa.

The Hana Highway may lead to Hana, but there's more beyond. The road now deteriorates considerably but scenery expands exponentially. Beyond Hana is the lower extent of **Haleakala National Park**. From mid-morning until late afternoon, you won't be alone at **Ohe`o Gulch**, often erroneously called the 'Seven Sacred' Pools, of which they're neither. There are actually a couple dozen pools, filled by a stream coming down Haleakala. Only the lower pools near the ocean are ever crowded. Take the **Waimoku Falls Trail** to the upper pools for privacy. But later... ah, later, towards sunset, all the pools empty of people. Then they indeed feel sacred, if not heavenly.

At the pools' ocean outlet is a large grassy area ending abruptly on high ocean cliffs. The stone remains of a fishing village are nearby. Forget swimming in the ocean: dangerous currents and sharks make the pools more inviting. You might stay here until sundown, with the pools to yourself, followed by dinner at the Hotel Hana-Maui. Driving the road back at night is no problem. And if a romantic moon smiles overhead, well then...

Above: beach babes; **right:** Ohe`o Gulch, Haleakala
Opposite: scenic Hana Highway

17: MOLOKAI AND LANAI *(see map, p69)*

Within sight of Maui are Molokai and Lanai, two quiet and slow-paced islands ideal for a day or longer, by boat or by plane. Choose just one per day.

Thought by ancient Polynesians to be ghost stomping grounds and thus best avoided, **Lanai's** red volcanic earth later proved fertile for pineapples, the economic backbone of this privately-owned island. But the island's corporate owners are shedding pineapples for tourism. Two new luxury hotels have appeared on Lanai: the **Manele Bay Hotel** with a Mediterranean-Hawaiian ambiance, and **The Lodge at Koele**, with fireplaces and an Old World character. Accessible by plane and boats from Maui, including ½-day snorkeling trips, Lanai is the perfect place to do nothing. Larger and geographically more diverse, **Molokai** is a good island for exploration. It has wide open grasslands, moody rain forests, and on the north shore, the world's tallest ocean cliffs.

Tour operators infest Hawaii, but there are two tours worth visiting Molokai alone for. The first is the **Molokai Wagon Ride** operated by a trio of lifetime Molokai residents. Beach time, grilled fish, an immense *heiau*, anecdotes, history, culture, guitar music, fruit yanked from handy trees, and sincerity all along the way.

The second tour humbles you with modern Hawaii's saddest but most graceful episode: Kalaupapa, the **former leprosy colony** on **Makanalua Peninsula**, isolated from the rest of Molokai by 2,000-ft (610-m) high cliffs and dangerous ocean waters. Starting in the early 1800s, Oahu health authorities shipped over 10,000 people – anybody with leprosy, now called Hansen's disease, and often those with nothing more than a bad skin rash – to Kalaupapa for a life sentence of exile. The 1873 arrival of Joseph De Veuster from Belgium, better known as Father Damien, brought civility and dignity to Kalaupapa. He later contracted and died of Hansen's disease. Protected by the National Park Service, the community has about 100 voluntary patients and residents.

Molokai and Lanai
6 miles / 10 km

Above: striking Molokai
Opposite: Father Damien's grave

Muleback Excursion

You can fly to Kalaupapa, or hike down the cliffside switchback trail, but the best bet is to join the **Molokai Mule Ride**. Permission is required to visit Molokai, but that's included as part of the muleback excursion. If you fly in or hike in, you'll still need an escort once

you reach Kalaupapa. Permission can be obtained through the state department of health in Honolulu or Molokai. Children under 16 are not allowed on the peninsula.

The best accommodation is **The Camps at Molokai Ranch**, three isolated campsites where accommodations are in first-rate 'tentalows,' a cross between spacious canvas-sided tents and bungalows, with a full range of activities and a centrally located clubhouse where meals are served.

For more sophisticated lodging **Kaluakoi Hotel & Golf Club** provides a resort-style alternative, with a golf course, tennis and watersports facilities.

molokai & lanai

Leisure
Activities

SHOPPING

Like eating, shopping is surely subjective. Some people flourish in large shopping centers and malls, others shrivel up within sight of one. Hawaii has huge shopping malls and small boutiques to suit all tastes. The island itineraries have highlighted some of the places to go, others are listed below.

There are a few things that make uniquely Hawaiian gifts, disregarding cheap souvenirs of baseball caps and coffee cups. The following are some of the more interesting gift suggestions:

Scrimshaw: the engraving of polished bone fossilized ivory with a sharp, pointed tool. Ink is then spread over the surface and absorbed only in the engraved lines. The result is a cross between an etching and tattoo. The art came into its own in the 1800s when bored sailors on whaling vessels scratched pictures on whale teeth. A number of non-endangered materials are now used, such as fossilized walrus tusk. The best buys are on Maui, in Lahaina and Ka`anapali.

Wood carvings: Handcrafted wood, most notably statuary (with the *tiki* as the theme), boxes and bowls made of koa, milo and other native woods, offer some of Hawaii's best-crafted *objets d'art*. Galleries and shops throughout the Hawaiian islands offer an impressive selection.

Kona coffee: Kona coffee plants originally came from Rio de Janeiro in the early 1800s. The plant grew well in several places in Hawaii, but flourished in South Kona, on the Big Island, which is where the only commercially-grown coffee in America now grows. It takes 500lb (227kg) of coffee beans to make 100lb (45kg) of processed coffee. Freshest on the Kona Coast, but sold throughout Hawaii at about the same prices.

**Ni`ihau shell lei:** Ni`ihau is a small, dry island west of Kauai, and privately owned by the wealthy Robinson family. A small community of about 250 Hawaiians live on the island, where Hawaiian is the language of education and the daily life of the people. Ni`ihau is *kapu* to visitors, ie off limits. Residents collect small, rare shells washed onto the beach and string them into necklaces of delicate colors. Very expensive. Best bought on Kauai at upscale galleries and jewelry stores.

Oahu

Ala Moana Center

Ala Moana Boulevard, between Waikiki and downtown Honolulu
Tel: 946 2811

Hawaii's largest shopping center, not to mention one of the largest open-air malls in the world, continues to grow, with Neiman Marcus among the newest additions, although not everything's upscale. It has about 200 stores covering 50 acres. Monday to Saturday 9.30am to 9pm; Sunday, 10am to 7pm.

Aloha Tower Marketplace

On Ala Moana Boulevard,
downtown Honolulu

Aloha Tower, Hawaii's tallest building when it was built in the 1920s, serves as a landmark presence at this complex of restaurants and shops. The mix of shops iincludes a number of shops focused on Hawaiiana.

Above: beads make a uniquely Hawaiian gift
Opposite: preparing heliconia blooms for sale

International Marketplace

2330 Kalakaua Avenue, Waikiki, across from Moana Hotel

Outdoors and casual. Bargaining is acceptable for anything and everything from gold jewelry and clothes to souvenirs and food. Casual restaurants. Open daily, 9am until midnight or later.

Kahala Mall

4211 Waialae Avenue, Honolulu
Tel: 732 7736

Oahu's nicest regional mall, anchored by big names such as Liberty House, Gap, Gap Kids, Barnes & Noble, and a collection of upscale shops and an eight-screen cineplex. Open 9am to 9pm.

Pearlridge Center

98–1005 Moanalua Drive, Pearlridge
Tel: 488 0981

Almost a match for Ala Moana in size, a monorail links its two phases. There's a fun mix of shops for the mall-addicted to appreciate as well as a large cineplex. Open 10am to 9pm.

Royal Hawaiian Shopping Center

2201 Kalakaua Avenue, Waikiki
Tel: 922 0588

This large open-air mall is Waikiki's biggest with more than 150 stores. Good for wandering if not buying. Open daily 9am to 10pm; Sunday to 9pm.

The Ward Centers

1050–1200 Ala Moana Boulevard across from Kewalo Basin
Tel: 591 8411

There are five separate components to this complex, including Ward Warehouse, Ward Center, and the Farmer's Market. The focus is on specialty shops including several galleries, dozens of wide-ranging stores and restaurants, with the Farmer's Market full of local color. Ward Center is mostly upscale, with a bookstore and several popular but semi-expensive restaurants. Open Monday to Friday, 10am to 9pm; Saturday and Sunday, 10am to 5pm.

Big Island

Keauhou Village Shopping Center

Off Kamehameha Avenue, in the Keauhou Resort
Tel: 322 5300

Convenient if you're staying in a nearby condo, with a supermarket and a selection of shops suited to both residents and visitors. Open 9am to 8pm.

Kona Inn Shops

On Ali`i Drive, Kailua-Kona
Tel: 329 6573

The oceanfront portion of the old Kona Inn is now a browser-friendly collection of restaurants and shops that is right in the heart of town. Open 9am to 9pm.

Lanihau Center
75–5595 Palani Road, Kailua-Kona
Tel: 329 9333
Kailua's largest mall has all the basics and a few specialty shops as well. Open daily, 9am to 6pm.

Prince Kuhio Plaza
111 E Puainako Street, Hilo 96720
Tel: 959 3555
Largest enclosed mall on the Big Island. Monday to Wednesday, Saturday, 9.30am to 5.30pm; Thursday and Friday, 9.30am to 9pm: Sunday, 10am to 4pm

The King's Shops at Waikoloa
Waikoloa Resort
Tel: 886 8811
An outdoor complex with shops and restaurants around a central mall with historic and cultural displays. Open 10am to 9pm.

Kauai

Coconut Marketplace
Between Wailua River and Kapa`a,
15 minutes north of Lihue
Tel: 822 3641
Standard tourist shopping mall with 70 outdoor shops. Open daily, 9am to 9pm.

Kilohana
Route 50, 2 miles west of Lihue
Tel: 245 5608
There are seven shops, including several interesting galleries, housed in a renovated Tudor-style home that was one of several

Wilcox family mansions on Kauai. Open daily, 9am to 6pm.

Kukui Grove
Junction of Route 50 and Nawiliwili Road
Tel: 245 7784
Kauai's largest mall with all the basics and some shops with visitor appeal. Open daily from 9am to 6pm.

Poipu Shopping Village
Poipu Road, Poipu
Tel: 742 2831
Resort shops, galleries and restaurants. Hawaiian entertainment through the week.

Maui

Front Street, Lahaina
Front Street, Lahaina
Front Street is home to Hawaii's greatest concentration of galleries as well as tasteful apparel and souvenir stores.

Ka`ahumanu Center
Ka`ahumanu Avenue, Kahului
Tel: 877 3333
Maui's largest mall is open-air, with a mix of department stores, a selection of specialty shops, restaurants and a cineplex.

Lahaina Cannery Mall
1221 Honoapiilani Highway,
north end of Lahaina
Tel: 661 5304
Mix of shops and fast food eateries, with schedule of Hawaiian entertainment. Open daily, 9.30am to 9.30pm.

The Shops at Kapalua
Kapalua Resort, Kapalua
Tel: 531 3000
A small outdoor complex adjacent to the Kapalua Bay Hotel.

Whalers Village
Kaanapali Beach
Tel: 661 4567
Over 50 shops from casual to upscale, plus two whaling museums. Open daily.

Above: kites galore
Opposite: Waikiki window shopping

EATING OUT

Hawaii's culinary offerings are bountiful, crossing over and blending into truly delightful experiences, like the increasingly-popular Pacific Rim cuisine. Yet one can also find pure ethnic food throughout the islands, especially from Asia and, of course, Italy. This listing is anything but comprehensive, and definitely not an effort to proclaim the *best* of Hawaii, for there are many more just as good, perhaps subjectively better. But these are all enjoyable in one way or another – for cuisine, presentation, atmosphere or experience. But like the stock market and love affairs, restaurants have their ups and downs. Serious eaters should buy the Zagat Hawaii Restaurant Survey, a little red book of restaurant evaluations. Three restaurant hot spots outside of Waikiki not covered below are Ward Center on Ala Moana Boulevard, Restaurant Row at Ala Moana and Punchbowl, and Aloha Tower Marketplace at Pier 1.

A price guide for a meal for two without drinks or tips is categorized as follows:

$ =   under US$30
$$ =   US$30–60
$$$ =   over US$60

Oahu

A Little Bit of Saigon
1160 Maunakea Street, Chinatown
Tel: 528 3663
Nothing fancy except the food: excellent and satisfying Vietnamese cuisine in a pleasant setting. $

Andy's (aka Manoa Health Market)
2904 East Manoa Road, Manoa Valley
Tel: 988 6161
Everything that Andy serves up from dawn to dusk is satisfying, whether it's one of his healthy sandwiches and green salads, or the brownies and muffins. Rustic seating. $

Arancino
255 Beachwalk
Tel: 923 5557
A casual eatery with deliciously prepared Northern Italian specialties at excellent prices. $–$$

Cafe Sistina
1314 S King Street, Honolulu
Tel: 596 0061
Milanese artist/chef Sergio Mitrotti has created a restaurant that's hip, with beautiful elements of the Sistine Chapel covering the walls, and a menu of specialties that are made to perfection. Good wine list too, and live music, mostly jazz on Friday and Saturday. $$–$$$

Caffélatte
339 Saratoga Road, Waikiki
Tel: 924 1414
At a quiet end of Waikiki, with open-air seating. Perfectly-served homemade pasta with unpronounceable but perfect sauces. $$$

Cheeseburger in Paradise
2500 Kalakaua Avenue, Waikiki
Tel: 923 3731
Made famous in Lahaina, now this is the place to go for Waikiki's best burgers. $–$$

David Paul's Diamond Head Grill
Colony Surf Hotel
Tel: 922 3734
Sophisticated ambiance and food to match, with a chanteuse or light jazz to accompany dinner. $$$

Duke's
2335 Kalakaua Avenue
Outrigger Waikiki Hotel
Tel: 922 2268

Above: upmarket flambé

The decor documents the life of Olympic-swimmer and surf legend, Duke Kahana-moku. Right on the beach, there's usually a young crowd, with weekend dancing and a party atmosphere. The food is good and setting unbeatable for a sense of place. *$$*

Hau Tree Lanai
New Otani Kaimana Beach Hotel
Tel: 923 1555
Breakfast, lunch and dinner with a beach-front setting and views of Waikiki. *$$–$$$*

Hoku
Kahala Mandarin Oriental
Tel: 734 2211
Chic multi-layer dining room with fish and seafood, steaks from a charcoal grill and wood-burning oven, and an oyster and sushi bar. *$$$*

Kacho
Waikiki Parc Hotel, Waikiki
Tel: 921 7272
Intimate Japanese restaurant with an emphasis on seafood and sushi. Fine Japanese dining requires serenity and imperceptible effort; Kacho excels at both. *$$–$$$*

Keo's Thai Cuisine
2028 Kuhio Avenue
Tel: 951 9355
It's hard not to mention Keo's: celebrities and locals drool over its Thai food. Keo's is part of an empire: there's another **Keo's** at Ward Center, and the original **Mekong**. *$$–$$$*

Orchids
Halekulani Hotel, Waikiki
Tel: 923 2311
Open to the ocean and romance. Service and food is excellent, as is Sunday's brunch, but starve the night before. *$$$*

Palomino's Euro-Bistro
55 Merchant Street, downtown
Tel: 528 2400
Great hip decor, with a contemporary deco feel well-suited to the delicious and inventive specialties on the menu. *$$–$$$*

Roy's Restaurant
6600 Kalanianaole Highway
Hawaii Kai
Tel: 396 7697
One of Honolulu's most popular Hawaiian regional cuisine restaurants. Problem: getting there through road-construction hell. *$$–$$$*

Ruth's Criss Steak House
500 Ala Moana Boulevard
Restaurant Row
Tel: 599 3860
The fact that this is a chain doesn't detract from the tender, delicious steaks that are served up. *$$$*

Sam Choy's Breakfast, Lunch & Crab
580 N Nimitz Highway Iwilei
Tel: 545 7979
My favorite of Hawaiian Regional chef Sam Choy's several eateries. The warehouse ambiance suits the pace of things, and the seafood is great. Fancier and closer to Waikiki is Sam Choy's Diamond Head Grill, at 449 Kapahulu Avenue, tel: 732 8645. *$$–$$$*

Left: imported cuisine

Sea Fortune
111 N King Street, Chinatown
Tel: 536 3822
Dim sum are the specialty of the house, and indeed they are well-priced and delicious, served by roving waiters with various options carried on hooded bamboo trays. *$–$$*

Big Island

Aloha Theater Cafe
Highway 11, Kainaliu
Tel: 322 3383

Diverse menu, from vegetarian to burgers to its decadent brownies. Best known for breakfasts outside on the terrace. *$*

Cafe Pesto
308 Kamehameha Avenue, Hilo
Tel: 969 6640
The atmosphere is casual, the service excellent, as are the pizzas and other Italian specialties. *$–$$*

Canoehouse
Mauna Lani Bay Hotel & Bungalows

Local Eats

To eat local and cheap without retreating to cheeseburgers, one must know what to ask for.

Dishes
bento: sometimes faithful to the Japanese original, sometimes localized beyond recognition. Great for picnics, with a little bit of everything: rice, pickled vegetables, meat or fish, and other curious things.
crackseed: seasoned seeds, including papaya, coconut, mango, pumpkin and watermelon.
huli huli chicken: if you drive past a park or grocery store parking lot and the air is filled with good-smelling smoke, it's huli huli chicken time – chicken cooked on a spit and sold in a bag.
malasada: from Portugal, much like a hole-less donut dipped in sugar.
manapua: Chinese steamed pastry with sweet pork and/or vegetables inside.
plate lunch: cheap and filling, with two scoop rice (*not* two scoops of rice) dished out with an ice cream scoop. A side scoop of macaroni salad, and some sort of meat on the rice. The variations are limitless and sometimes even interesting.
poi: pounded taro plant root, mixed with water into a thick paste. Said to be nutritious but it's something of, um, an acquired taste.
pupu: Called an hors d'oeuvre elsewhere,

pupus are properly eaten with a flower-garnished tropical drink and a blossoming sunset on the horizon.
shave ice: those not in the know call these shaved ice, or worse, snow cones; this is akin to calling mousse a whipped pudding. Ice is shaved off a block in fine slivers, packed just right in a paper cone and topped with one or more sugar syrups. Connoisseurs request sweet *azuki* beans at the bottom, perhaps with vanilla ice cream, too.
saimin: looking like a bowl of noodles found anywhere in Asia, that's what it is, Hawaiian style. Includes fishcake, green onions, vegetables, maybe some bits of meat and other things in the broth.

Fish
ahi: yellowfin tuna. Widely used in Hawaii, including for sushi and sashimi.
aku: Skipjack tuna. Heavier than *ahi*.
mahimahi: dolphin gamefish, not the mammal. Ubiquitous in Hawaii, mild-tasting and usually grilled or baked. So popular it often must be imported. Ask for fresh, not frozen.
ono: wahoo, or king mackerel. Seasonal in autumn and winter. Popular in most restaurants.
opakapaka: pink snapper. Used in upscale restaurants.
uku: grey or deep-sea snapper, excellent broiled, fried or baked.

South Kohala
Tel: 885 6622
Has a reputation for its appealing ambiance and creative Pacific Rim menu. The restaurant name defines the decor. *$$–$$$*

Jameson's by the Sea
77–6452 Ali`i Drive, Kailua-Kona
Tel: 329 3195
Romantic and on the beach, nearly perfect seafood, especially local fish and smoked salmon. American fare too. Delicious setting at sunset. *$$*

Le Soleil
Mauna Lani Bay Hotel & Bungalows
South Kohala
Tel: 885 6622
Sophisticated and romantic French and Continental dinners. Outstanding wine list and attention to detail. Jacket required. *$$$*

Merriman's
Highway 19, Waimea
Tel: 885 6822
People drive and fly to Waimea for Merriman's incredible Pacific Rim and local menu. Highly-regarded throughout Hawaii. *$$–$$$*

Sibu Cafe
75–5695 Ali`i Drive, Kona
Tel: 329 1112
Purveyor of good Southeast Asian dishes, without pretense. Popular for its Indonesian food and ambiance. *$*

Kauai

A Pacific Cafe
4831 Kuhio Highway, Kapa`a
Tel: 822 0013
Consistently receives high marks from locals, even competitors. Prices match its upscale but easy-going surroundings. Asian and Pacific Rim food. *$$–$$$*

Brennecke's Beach Broiler
2100 Hoone Road, Poipu Beach
Tel: 742 7588
Across the street from the beach and on the

mark for food – seafood, beef, burgers and a big salad bar. A solid venue for people and sunset watching. Beach sandals required. *$–$$*

Casa di Amici
2484 Keneke Road, Kilauea
Tel: 828 1555
Worth a drive for dinner, this nice little restaurant has well-prepared pasta topped with a wide variety of sauces. Open-air seating, with intimate music in the evenings. *$$*

Gaylord's
Kilohana, in Puhi
Tel: 245 9593
In an open courtyard at a 1930s plantation-era estate mansion that offers lovely views, Gaylord's is a requisite stop on a culinary tour of the islands. Somewhat pricey menu. *$$–$$$*

Hanalei Gourmet
5–5161 Kuhio Highway, Hanalei
Tel: 826 2524
Located in the old Hanalei schoolhouse, the food is excellent, and there's entertainment on select evenings. *$–$$*

Hanamaulu Restaurant & Tea House
3–4291 Kuhio Highway, Hanamaulu
Tel: 245 2511
Japanese-style teahouse seating, with a menu that ranges from sushi to tempura to Chinese specialties in generous portions. *$–$$*

La Cascata
Princeville Hotel, near Hanalei
Tel: 826 2761

Above: magnificent Gaylord's at Kilohana

Mediterranean atmosphere, right down to the tall windows that swing open to the outside. Its fine cuisine extends considerably beyond the usual pasta. Romantic. *$$$*

Maui

David Paul's Lahaina Grill
Lahaina Hotel,
127 Lahainaluna Road, Lahaina
Tel: 667 5117
This beautifully renovated place is among the best and most in vogue. Innovative Pacific Rim menu. Sophisticated but relaxed. *$$–$$$*

Gerard's
The Plantation Inn,
174 Lahainaluna Road, Lahaina
Tel: 661 8939
Expensive and chic, romantic and relaxing – there's pleasure in its wide-ranging French cuisine. Outdoor seating on the lanai, or indoors. *$$–$$$*

Hailimaile General Store
Hailimaile Road, Hailimaile
Tel: 572 2666
Great atmosphere, friendly service, and Pacific Rim specialties that make this a Maui favorite. *$$–$$$*

Jacques Bistro
89 Hana Highway, Pa`ia
Tel: 579 6255
The waitresses are very obviously chosen for their good looks, which is a perfect complement to great food at great prices. *$$*

Longhi's
888 Front Street, Lahaina
Tel: 667 2288
Eccentric for its walking-and-talking menus, Longhi's has a solid reputation, including people-watching. American and Italian fare. *$$–$$$*

Mama's Fish House
Highway 36, Kuau, near Pa`ia
Tel: 579 8488
One of those places that excels without trumpeting its success. A wonderful spot right on the ocean, it has, what some say, Maui's best fish. Those in the know, go. *$$–$$$*

Plantation House
Kapalua Plantation Golf Course Clubhouse
Tel: 669 6299
The feel is country club chic, with Hawaiian-themed art work on the walls, open-air views, friendly service and an extensive menu with Pacific Rim specialties. *$$–$$$*

Saeng's Thai Cuisine
2119 Vineyard Street, Wailuku
Tel: 244 1568
Thai food in a bright, quiet ambiance, especially in the garden. Food and service is excellent. Nearby is **Siam Thai Cuisine**, with good food but lacking in atmosphere. *$$*

Sansei
Kapalua Shops, Kapalua
Tel: 669 6286
Japanese cuisine at its best with a wide-ranging menu with real taste-appeal. *$$$*

The Pacific Grill
Four Seasons Resort, Wailea,
South Maui
Tel: 874 8000
Breakfast, lunch and dinner – there's simply nothing less than perfect here. Perhaps the best of Pacific Rim menus, and ocean views, too. *$$–$$$*

Above: a great way to meet the locals

ACTIVITIES

Beaches

It's impossible to list all of Hawaii's beaches. Those that follow are but a few of many nice ones. Not all of them are necessarily good swimming beaches, but there's more to a beach than just swimming – sunbathing, canoeing, picnic, camping, scenery and people-watching come to mind.

Coral injuries, even the small nip, infect easily and heal slowly. If there is reason to worry about sharks, you'll know. Don't turn your back on waves, especially in winter. Windward beaches occasionally have jellyfish invasions; watch for golf-ball-size, purplish man-of-wars on the sand and in the water. Finally, Hawaii's beaches undergo radical personality changes from season to season. North shore beaches are usually glass-smooth in summer, but viciously rough in winter. Use your head, follow the warnings, and ask the lifeguard.

Oahu

Sandy Beach: Fantastic sun, sand, setting, and people watching. But the water is always unpredictable, seasonally dangerous. *Always check with lifeguards*, even when people are in the water; they're probably expert body surfers, and Sandy's their turf. Full facilities.

Waimanalo: Safe beach all year, with lush and dramatic scenery. One of Hawaii's longest beaches, with a gentle, shallow bottom. Weekdays the beach is nearly always empty; weekends bring out the canoe clubs, baseball practice, and families. Full facilities and picnic areas.

Kailua Beach: Miles of powder-white sands and calm, turquoise waters make this a year-round recommend for swimming, kayaking, and windsurfing, although the snorkeling is only so-so.

Malaekahana: Not so popular, not so typical but quite a beautiful beach. Large groves of ironwood trees, with campgrounds and full facilities. The water is usually calm, clear, and excellent for swimming, especially for children.

Waimea Bay: Glass-smooth in summer for perfect swimming and snorkeling – but come winter, the bay is explosive and suitable only for world-class surfers. A small but beautiful beach; full facilities and lifeguards. Exciting in winter, sleepy in summer.

Big Island

Spencer Beach Park: In the shadow of a powerful temple to the war god, this is a popular local beach, perfect for families with children; snorkeling and swimming are good, but of course, the sunsets are better. Full facilities.

Kauna`oa Beach, aka Mauna Kea Beach Resort: A graceful crescent of sand, this is one of the Big Island's finest beaches. Although the Mauna Kea Hotel dominates it, the beach is public, with showers and restrooms at the southern end. Great swimming and snorkeling.

Hapuna Beach: A long white-sand beach that would be excellent on any island, but on this beach-short island, Hapuna is stupendous. Full facilities. Sun is guaranteed anytime except night. Full picnicking and camping facilities. Good for winter whale-watching.

Kealakekua Bay: Not much of a beach here, but adequate. Historically the area is interesting: a *heiau* hunkers nearby and Captain Cook made his final splash down the way. The bay is a state underwater park, meaning it has good snorkeling. Full facilities.

Kauai

Polihale: Kauai's remotest beach but still easily reached by car – just drive to the end of the road. This is the western end of the Na

Right: surf's up

Pali Coast, and the cliffs that flank the beach's northeast end are impressive. Wild – use common sense. Facilities, no lifeguard.

Poipu: Good play area: swimming, snorkeling, picnics, sand castles. Bodysurfers thrive at nearby Brennecke Beach. Close to the resorts and thus sometimes crowded. The Poipu Beach area is quite nice and beautiful, good area for children. Full facilities.

Hanalei: Kauai's best beaches are on the North Shore, not always swimmable but always spectacular and moody. Hanalei Bay Beach is wide and arcing, seeming to continue forever. Summer swimming is excellent, but winter is dangerous and best avoided.

Lumaha`i: Often photographed from an overlook, this North Shore beach is better experienced down on the sand, where filming for *South Pacific* took place. The safest swimming spot is on the Hanalei Bay side; the currents here are tricky. No lifeguards.

Ha`ena/Ke`e: Used for the mystical Bali Hai in the film *South Pacific*. Most of the time, forget swimming at Ha`ena, but take in the scenery. Ke`e Beach, at the end of the road, is good for swimming and snorkeling in summer. Winters – uncork the wine and watch the pounders.

Maui

Kapalua: This beach is a simply superb beach, almost perfect in many ways, with good snorkeling and relaxing. A local favorite. Facilities. There can be some confusion with Fleming Beach nearby.

Ka`anapali: Maui's most famous beach and resort area. Two mile-long stretches of fine sand and good swimming. Watch for the red flags signalling dangerous conditions. Has a sandy bottom that drops quickly. Good place to strut.

Wailea: Encompasses five beaches – Keawakapu, Mokapu, Ulua, Wailea, and Polo. Smooth and sandy bottoms. Public facilities are not always handy, but the sun certainly is. Ulua Beach is probably the most popular, with good bodysurfing, snorkeling. Up the coast in Kihei, **Kama`ole Beaches I, II,** and **III** are good.

Ho`okipa: On the opposite coast from Maui's great resort beaches, this is a beach with great spectator activity: world-class windsurfing. Swimming: occasionally good. Full facilities including grills and picnic areas.

Golf

Hawaii's golf courses are popular with North Americans and Asians year round. Plan ahead. Two sources of comprehensive information are *Hawaii Golf Map* and the *Hawaii Golf Guide*.

Information on the golf courses is listed in this order: *number of holes, par, clubhouse (C), driving range (DR), approximate fees ($ = under US$40; $$ = US$40–80; $$$ = over US$80), and Golf Digest rating.* All listed courses are public.

Big Island

Hilo Municipal Golf Course
Hilo. Tel: 959 7711
18 71 DR *$*

Mauna Kea Beach Golf Club
South Kohala. Tel: 882 7222
18 72 C DR *$$$* GD: #3

Mauna Lani Resort
South Kohala. Tel: 885 6655
Two courses: 18 72/72 C DR *$$$*
Naniloa Country Club
Hilo. Tel: 935 3000
9 35 C DR *$*
Volcano Golf and Country Club
Volcano. Tel: 967 7331
18 72 C *$$*
Waikoloa Beach Golf Club
South Kohala. Tel: 885 6060
18 70 C DR *$$$*
Waikoloa Kings Course
South Kohala. Tel: 886 7888
18 72 C DR *$$$* GD: #4

Maui and Molokai
Ka`anapali Golf Course
West Maui. Tel: 661 3691
Two courses: 18 71/71 DR *$$$*
Kaluakoi Golf Club
Molokai Island. Tel: 552 2739
18 72 C DR *$$*
Kapalua Golf Club
West Maui. Tel: 669 8044
Three courses: 18 71/72/73 DR *$$$* GD: #6
and #7
Makena Golf Club
South Maui. Tel: 879 3344
Two courses: 18 72/72 C DR *$$$*
Sandalwood Golf Course
Waikapu, West Maui. Tel: 242 4653
18/72 DR *$$$*
Wailea Golf Club
South Maui. Tel: 879 2966
Three courses: 72/72/72 C DR *$$$*

Oahu
Ala Wai Golf Course
Honolulu. Tel: 734 3656
18 70 C DR *$*
Ranks world's busiest course by Guinness
Book of Records.
Hawaii Kai Golf Course
East Honolulu. Tel: 395 2358
Two courses: 18 72/54 C DR *$$*
Ko`olau Golf Club
Windward Oahu
18/72 DR *$$$*
Scenic. Rated Hawaii's most difficult.

Ko Olina Golf Club
West Oahu. Tel: 676 5309
18 72 C DR *$$$* GD: #9
Makaha Golf Club
West Oahu. Tel: 695 9544
18 72 DR *$$$* GD: #8
Makaha Valley Country Club
West Oahu. Tel: 695 9578
18 71 DR *$$*
Olomana Golf Links
Waimanalo. Tel: 259 7926
18 72 C DR *$*
The Links at Kuilima
North Shore. Tel: 293 8574
18 72 C DR *$$$*

Kauai
Kauai Lagoons Resort
Lihue. Tel: 241 6000
Two courses: 18 72/72 C DR *$$$*
GD: #2
Kiahuna Golf Club
Poipu. Tel: 742 9595
18 70 C DR *$$*
Poipu Bay Resort Golf Course
Poipu. Tel: 742 9489
18 72 C DR *$$*
Prince Golf & Country Club
Princeville/North Shore. Tel: 826 5000
18 72 C DR *$$$* GD: #1
Princeville Makai Golf Course
Princeville/North Shore. Tel: 826 3580
Three courses: 27 72 C DR *$$*
GD: #5
Wailua Municipal Golf Course
Kapa`a. Tel: 241 6666
18 72 C DR *$*

Raft Excursions

Kauai and Big Island
Na Pali Explorer
PO Box 576, `Ele`ele, 96705
Toll: (800) 852 4183
Kauai. Tel: 335 9909

Diving

Some dive shops are like factories: On Oahu,
a lot of them are found in the Waikiki area,

Opposite: beachside stroll at Wailea

catering mainly to tourists. The shops listed here cater to both locals and tourists.

Kauai
Fathom Five Divers *Tel: 742 6991*
Sea Sport Divers *Tel: 742 9303*

Oahu
Aaron's Dive Shop *Tel: 262 2333*

Big Island
Kona Coast Divers *Tel: 329 8802*
Big Island Divers *Tel: 329 6068*

Maui
Lahaina Divers *Tel: 661 4505*
Scuba Shaek *Tel: 661 5555*

Kayaking
Oahu
Kayak Oahu Adventures
Tel: 923 0539

Kauai
Island Adventures
Tel: 245 9662

Outfitters Kauai
Tel: 742 9887

Maui
Maui Sea Kayaking
Tel: 572 6229

Big Island
Ocean Safari's Kayak Adventures
Tel: 326 4699

Helicopters

Big Island
Mauna Kea Helicopters *Tel: 885 6400*
Volcano Heli-Tours *Tel: 967 7578*

Kauai
Hawaii Helicopters
Tel: 826 6591 Toll: (800) 367 7095
`Ohana Helicopter Tours
Tel: 245 3996 Toll: (800) 222 6989

Maui
Blue Hawaiian Helicopters
Tel: 871 8844 Toll: (800) 745 2583
Sunshine Helicopters
Tel: 871 0722 Toll: (800) 544 2520
Hawaii Helicopters
Tel: 877 3900 Toll: (800) 994 9099

Gliding
Oahu
Soar Hawaii
North Shore, Oahu. Tel: 637 3147
The Original Glider Rides
North Shore, Oahu. Tel: 677 3404

Hang-Gliding
Maui
Hang Gliding Maui
Tel: 572 6557

Kauai
Birds in Paradise
Tel: 822 5309

Hiking / Walking Tours
Oahu
Oahu Nature Tours
Tel: 924 2473 Toll: (800) 861 6108
Passport Hawaii
Tel: 943 0371

Big Island
Hawaii Forest & Trail
Kailua-Kona. Tel: 322 8881
Toll: (800) 464 1993

Right: diver's delight

NIGHTLIFE

Perhaps I'm old-fashioned, but my idea of nightlife in Hawaii is romance on the beach, by starlight or moonlight, and a bottle of wine, with no sounds but the roll of the ocean and the liquid poetry of my sweet talk. There are those who'll take that moonlight stroll, and still want something high energy to do. Here are some suggestions for shows and dancing. Outside of Honolulu, the pickings are thin, at least by mainland standards. After all, there are all those beaches...

Oahu
Aloha Tower Marketplace
Piers 8, 9 and 10 at Aloha Tower, Honolulu
Tel: 528 5700
This is Honolulu's hippest hangout. The harborside setting has appeal, with a mix of shops, kiosks and restaurants to choose from. Check out Don Ho's Island Grill (tel: 528 0807), where this Hawaiian icon is memorialized with period piece decor. The Brothers Cazimero (tel: 847 6353), a stellar duo of Hawaiian music, perform on Saturday nights with a cocktail and dinner show.

Anna Bannana's
2440 South Beretania Street, Honolulu
Tel: 946 5190
Hip hangout for years with energetic bands, playing anything from reggae to rock 'n roll. Near the University of Hawaii, and thus attracts young crowds. Dancing and no dress code. There is live music from 9pm to 2am.

Creation: A Polynesian Odyssey
Princess Kaiulani Hotel
120 Kaiulani Avenue
Tel: 922 5811
The story of creation from the Polynesian perspective, done with chants, music and dance that have the ring of cultural authenticity. Cocktail and dinner shows nightly.

Frank De Lima
Outrigger Reef Towers Hotel,
227 Lewers Street, Waikiki
Tel: 923 9861
Very talented, very funny, very irreverent comedian. Popular with locals, cutting nobody any slack. Sometimes features guest artistes. The dinner show is highly recommended, but make reservations in advance. Nightly, from Tuesday to Saturday, 9pm.

House Without A Key
Halekulani Hotel, Waikiki. Tel: 923 2311
An outdoor patio with classic Diamond Head views provides a setting for Hawaiian music and hula.

Magic of Polynesia
Waikiki Beachcomber Hotel
2300 Kalakaua Avenue
Tel: 922 4646
An impressive Las Vegas-style extravaganza of special effects, illusions and kitsch Hawaiiana by master illusionist John Hirokawa. Nightly cocktail and dinner shows.

The Don Ho Show
Waikiki Beachcomber Hotel
2300 Kalakaua Avenue
Tel: 922 4646
The ultimate Hawaiian crooner continues to wow 'em with a show that's casual, funny, and full of aloha. Cocktail and dinner shows Sunday through Thursday.

Wave Waikiki
1877 Kalakaua Avenue, Honolulu
Tel: 941 0424
Long-time pop music venue for local and visiting bands. Dancing or drinking. Daily, 9pm to 4am.

Above: a sunset to worship at Kaupo

Big Island

Cronie's
11 Waianuenue Avenue, Hilo
Tel: 935 5158
A bar and restaurant with plenty of local color. There's Hawaiian music from 5pm to 7pm on Tuesday, Thursday and Friday. After 7pm, the beat goes contemporary.

Eclipse Restaurant
75–5711 Kuakini Hwy, Kailua
Tel: 329 4686
The disco tunes start up at 10pm, Friday through Sunday.

Kauai

Gilligan's
Outrigger Kauai Beach Hotel, Lihue
Tel: 245 1955
Open Thursday through Saturday nights, 8pm to 4am for music and dancing.

The Library
Princeville Resort
Tel: 826 9644
Soothing piano in an elegant setting makes this a great recommend.

Maui

Hapa's Brew Haus
41 E Lipoa Street, Kihei
Tel: 879 9001

There's live music throughout the week at this microbrewery where the food is Italian despite the German-sounding name.

Moose Mcgillycuddy's
844 Front Street, Lahaina
Tel: 667 7758
There's lots of nightlife in Lahaina, but when it comes to dancing, the Moose reigns supreme. Serves good sandwiches, burgers and salads too.

Tsunami
Grand Wailea Resort Hotel & Spa,
South Maui
Tel: 875 1234
The name says it all: tidal wave. High-class, high-power music and dancing in Wailea. Call for hours.

Luaus

Luaus – a unique form of Hawaiian nightlife that ususally begins at sundown – range from the tacky to the nearly authentic. But, like most first-time visitors to Hawaii, you'll probably have fun at any, or all, of them. And the heart of any luau still continues to be the preparation and unearthing of the underground rock oven. Most resort hotels organize some sort of luau night with entertainment or a Polynesian revue with drums, fire dancers, and shimmering *hula* dancers. Advance reservations are required. Luaus are expensive, from US$40–50 per adult – but you won't eat for a week afterwards, making it a real bargain.

Oahu

Chuck Machado's Waikiki Beach Luau
Waikiki
Tel: 951 9990
Toll: (800) 367 5255
Nightly at 5.30pm.

Germaine's Luau
Ko Olina Resort
Tel: 949 4218
A 40-minute motorcoach run from Waikiki, departing nightly at 5pm.

Above: tropical-style liquid sustenance

Paradise Cove
West Oahu. Tel: 973 LUAU
Nightly 5pm. Lots to do and a big crowd to share it with.

Royal Hawaiian Luau
Royal Hawaiian Hotel, Waikiki
Tel: 923 7311
Friday at 6pm. The 'Pink Palace of the Pacific' as it is known, with its familiar coral-pink stucco and Moorish-Spanish design, is the home of Waikiki's only beachfront luau.

The Polynesian Cultural Center
North Shore
Tel: 293 3333
The Ali`i Luau is one way to end a visit to this cultural attraction. Nightly, except Sunday, at 5pm.

Big Island
Island Breeze Luau
King Kamehameha Hotel, Kailua
Tel: 326 4969
Sunday, Tuesday, Wednesday and Thursday at 5.30pm.

Kona Village Resort
South Kohala, Big Island
Tel: 325 5555
The feel is family friendly, the food is good. Friday at 6.15pm.

Mauna Kea Resort Luau
Mauna Kea Beach Hotel
Tel: 882 7222
Tuesday at 5.30pm.

Kauai
Drums of Paradise
Hyatt Regency Kauai, Poipu
Tel: 742 1234
Sunday and Thursday at 6pm.

Kauai Coconut Beach Resort
Kapaa, Kauai. Tel: 822 3455
Great central location in Kapaa. In a setting under the palms. Nightly at 5.30pm. There is also a nightly torchlighting ceremony.

Smith's Tropical Paradise
Wailua. Tel: 821 6895
30 acres and family feeling. Monday, Wednesday and Friday at 5pm.

Maui
Rennaisance Wailea Beach Resort
Wailea, South Maui. Tel: 879 4900
Located on pristine Mokapu Beach in Wailea. Thursday, 6pm.

Royal Lahaina Luau
Ka`anapali
Tel: 661 3611
A beachside setting accompanied by sunset. Nightly at 5pm.

Old Lahaina Luau
1251 Front Street, Lahaina, Maui
Tel: 667 1998
Perhaps the best of them all, with authenticity, aloha and good food in abundance. Nightly at 5.30pm.

Dinner Cruises
Oahu
Navatek I
2270 Kalakaua Avenue, Waikiki
Tel: 924 1515 Toll: (800) 852 4183
Departs Kewalo basin, with bus transfers from Waikiki provided. Three levels of dining and entertainment in a state-of-the-art ship that provides comfortable travel even when seas are choppy.

Big Island
Captain Beans' Cruises
Kailua-Kona
Tel: 329 1688 Toll: (800) 831 5541
Departs Kailua Pier and cruises the Kona Coast.

Kauai
Na Pali Explorer
Port Allen
Tel: 335 9909 Toll: (800) 852 4183
Sunset, dinner and entertainment along the Na Pali Coast, aboard the fast and steady Navatek II.

CALENDAR OF EVENTS

January

Third week: Narcissus Queen Pageant. Held in Honolulu, this is part of the **Narcissus Festival**, continuing throughout February. A celebration of the Chinese New Year; includes a pageant, a coronation ball, Chinese cultural demonstrations and festivities with lion dances and food. Tel: 533 3181.

Third week: Annual Ala Wai Canoe Challenge. A no-experience-necessary canoe race down the Ala Wai Canal, Waikiki. Tel: 923 1802.

Last week: Molokai Makahiki. Friendly Isle Festival featuring hula performances, art and crafts, games and food. Kaunakakai Molokai. Tel: 553 3876.

February

Continuation of **Narcissus Festival**, from third week January.

Third week: Annual Buffalo's Big Board Surfing Classic. Indeed a classic, with old-timers competing on old-fashioned wooden surfboards – the big boards. Hawaiian entertainment and food. Makaha Beach, Oahu. Tel: 525 8090.

Third week: Waimea Town Celebration. A big 2-day town party with the usual festivities: food, entertainment, parade, games, races. Waimea, Kauai. Tel: 338 9957.

March

First week: Cherry Blossom Festival. A Japanese cultural celebration held at Kapiolani Park, Waikiki. Includes traditional and contemporary Japanese entertainment, demonstrations, and *mochi* (rice) pounding. Tel: 949 2255.

Variable: Hawaii Ski Cup Open. International and club snow ski races. The date depends on snow conditions. On the top of Mauna Kea, Big Island. Tel: 737 4394.

Last week: Prince Kuhio Festival. A celebration of Prince Jonah Kuhio Kalanianaole. Canoe races, royal ball, pageant, period music and dances, and a commemorative service. At Prince Kuhio Park, Poipu, Kauai. Tel: 245 3971. Also on other islands.

March 26: Prince Kuhio Day. State holiday in honor of Prince Jonah Kuhio Kalanianaole.

April

Easter: Merrie Monarch Festival. The best of all the hula competitions, which concludes a week of celebration in honor of King Kalakaua. Hilo, on the Big Island. Tel: 935 9168. Alert: Hotel rooms are nearly impossible to book at the last minute in Hilo during the festival so make sure that you plan way ahead.

May

First week: Annual Lei Day Celebration. Cultural shows by elementary school students, statewide lei competitions, exhibitions and the Lei Queen coronation. Kapiolani Park, Waikiki. Tel: 266 7654. Celebrations also held on the neighboring islands.

June

First and second week: King Kamehameha Celebrations. Statewide festivities honoring Hawaii's first monarch. Includes the lei-draping ceremony of King Kamehameha statues in Honolulu and the Big Island, and floral parades and hula.

June 11: Kamehameha Day. A state holiday.

July

Variable: Annual Makawao Rodeo and Parade. Probably the best of all Hawaii rodeos, and certainly its liveliest. Makawao, Maui. Tel: 572 9928.

Third week: Hale`iwa Bon Odori Festival. A cheerful Buddhist festival of the dead. Bon dances and a floating lantern ceremony. Highly recommended. Tel: 637 4382.

Third week: Kapalua Wine Symposium. Experts gather for seminars and tasting. Kapalua Bay Hotel, West Maui. Tel: 669 0244.

Third and fourth week: Koloa Plantation Days. A week of festivities celebrating the

Opposite: outrigger canoe paddlers show their style

start of sugar plantations in Hawaii. Koloa, Kauai. Tel: 332 9201.

August

Variable: Annual Hawaiian International Billfish Tournament. The premier international marlin fishing contest. Kailua-Kona, Big Island. Tel: 836 0974.

First week: Queen Lili`uokalani Keiki Hula Competition. Young boys and girls from hula schools compete in both modern and ancient hula. Oahu. Tel: 521 6905.

September

Mid-September through October: Aloha Festivals. In honor of the times of the Hawaiian monarchy with street parties, canoe races and parades. Dates vary widely from island to island. Tel: 944 8857.

October

First and second week: Winter League Baseball. Baseball fans can check out pro baseball's top minor league prospects and international stars in action. Teams include Honolulu Sharks, West Oahu Canefires, Maui Stingrays and Hilo Stars. Season runs through mid-December. Tel: 973 7247.

Variable: Ironman Triathlon World Championships. *The* race of the world: 2½-mile swim, 112-mile bicycle ride, and a 26-mile run. Kailua-Kona, Big Island. Tel: 329 0063.

November

Variable, through December: Triple Crown of Surfing. Concludes the professional world tour of surfing. North Shore, Oahu. Tel: 377 5850.

Variable, through December: Hawaii International Film Festival. Showcases the best of films from throughout Asia, the Pacific, and the Americas. Tel: 944 7707.

December

December 7: Pearl Harbor Day. In memory of those who were killed during the Japanese bombing of Oahu on December 7, 1941, a memorial service is held at the USS Arizona Memorial.

Second week: Annual Honolulu Marathon. International competitors gather in Oahu. Tel: 734 7200.

Variable: Honolulu Marathon. One morning every December thousands of runners from all over the world set off from the Aloha Tower on a 26-mile, 385-yard marathon course along Oahu's south shore.

Practical Information

GETTING THERE

By Air

There are only three practical ways of arriving in Hawaii: by private boat, cruise ship, or, for most of us, by commercial flights.

International and US domestic flights arrive at and depart from the Honolulu International Airport, Kahului, Maui, and Kona on the Big Island. North American gateway cities include Los Angeles, San Francisco, Seattle and Vancouver. International gateway cities – primarily from Asia – include Tokyo, Taipei, Hong Kong, Manila and Sydney.

Making a transfer in Honolulu from an international/mainland flight to an inter-island one is easy as both terminals are at the same airport but housed in separate buildings. Shuttle buses are available.

Note: If going to Waikiki, don't rent a car at the airport and drive. Take a taxi. There is no direct and easy way from the airport to Waikiki. Pick up a rental car in Waikiki. Also, don't plan on taking the public bus that departs frequently from Honolulu airport to Waikiki: luggage cannot be brought on board. Airport, tel: 836 6411.

TRAVEL ESSENTIALS

When to Visit

Anytime, of course. However, there are two peak tourist seasons: June through August and December through February. Reservations for peak periods should be made in advance.

Visas and Passports

Entry requirements and restrictions are exactly the same as for anywhere else in the United States. Canadians don't require a passport.

Vaccinations

None needed. But forget your pet, as all animals must be quarantined for a minimum of 4 months on arrival in Hawaii.

Weather

There are two seasons: warm and less warm. It's warmest from April until November, but nearly-constant trade winds keep humidity down. August and September are the hottest, and sometimes humid. December through February is coolest but these are also the months when rain is the heaviest, although it rains nearly everyday somewhere on each island. Weather varies widely from island to island, and on an island itself. If it's rainy in one place, it's usually sunny somewhere else on the island.

Trade winds are usually from the northeast. The windward side of an island – the northeast side – is wettest and greenest. Leeward sides are drier and sunnier. When the northeast trades stop, southerly winds often take over, called kona winds. Hot and humid weather follows; fortunately, kona winds are rare in summer. Weather information, tel: 833 2849.

Clothing

Casual and light, nearly always. No neckties, but a sports jacket is required at some restaurants. Bring a light jacket or sweater for cool winter evenings and higher elevations.

Above: rainbow across the sea
Opposite: gliding along Kauai's Na Pali Coast

Electricity

Standard US 110–120 volt, 60 cycle AC.

Time Differences

Same day as mainland North America, one day behind Asia. Time is two hours behind Los Angeles, five hours behind New York, 10 hours behind London. Hawaii does not shift to summer daylight savings time.

GETTING ACQUAINTED

Geography

The Hawaiian Island chain extends 1,523 miles (2,437km) southeast to northwest, from the Big Island to Kure Atoll, near Midway. Don't make a common mistake: Hawaii is not in the South Pacific. Hawaii is above the equator, far north of Tahiti, and on the same latitude as Mexico City and Hong Kong. There are eight main islands, all in the chain's southeastern part: Hawaii (aka Big Island), Maui, Kaho`olawe (uninhabited), Lanai, Molokai, Oahu, Kauai and Ni`ihau. Two islands, Lanai and Ni`ihau, are private and closed to visitors. Total land area is 6,425sq miles (16,640sq km), two-thirds of that belonging to the Big Island.

Government and Economy

State executive powers are constitutionally vested in a governor and lieutenant governor, elected every four years. A bicameral legislature meets yearly in Hawaii's capital, Honolulu. Hawaii's government exists only on two levels: state and county. There is one combined city and county jurisdiction, Honolulu, including Oahu and the islands not within the three other non-metropolitan jurisdictions, or counties, of Hawaii, Maui and Kauai.

Economically, the per capita buying power in Hawaii is quite low; the cost of living is second highest in the United States. Sugar and pineapple were once modern Hawaii's economic base. Tourism is now number one, with 7 million visitors in 1990 bringing US$9.4 billion to Hawaii. The American military presence adds substantially to Hawaii's economy.

Religion

Catholic, Protestant, Mormon, Buddhist.

How Not to Offend

Easy: remember that Hawaii is neither a theme park nor a fantasy island. Rather, it is home for a million people, with their own lifestyles and expectations. Don't judge people and lifestyles by Western standards. Hawaii is as much Asian and Pacific as it is American and European, a fact easily forgotten by visitors. Hawaii is friendly and gracious, but it runs on island time. Other suggestions:

• Don't try to speak or mimic the local English patois, usually called pidgin English. Only a true *kama`aina* can speak it properly. Visitors and newcomers trying to speak it sound ridiculous and even mocking.

• Don't ever honk your car's horn; it's considered terribly rude and unnecessary.

• Don't lean on old cars; it belongs to someone, and under that paint could be nothing but rust. You might put a hole in the car. No joke.

• Don't wear his-and-her matching Hawaiian shirts and/or muumuus. Actually, no one is offended by this, but you'll spare yourself some snickers.

Whom Do You Trust

Almost everybody. Honolulu, for example, is one of the safest cities in the United States. Most problems, when they occur, are with unattended rental cars at beach and lookout parking lots. Lock the car and don't leave valuables in view.

Above: having a great time

Population

Statewide: 1,108,229. About 80 percent reside on Oahu. Descending order of population: Caucasian, Japanese, Filipino, Chinese, Black, Korean, Hawaiian, Samoan and Puerto Rican.

MONEY MATTERS

Currency

Standard US currency and coins in all the usual denominations. $1=100 cents.

Credit Cards

All internationally-popular cards accepted: American Express, Visa, MasterCard, and to a lesser degree, Diners Club. Essential for car rental.

Cash Machines

Everywhere – at bank branches and shopping centers – and accessible 24hrs daily. Bank of Hawaii's machines are the most universal, accepting a range of cards.

Tippng

Yes, for food and drinks, taxis, baggage porters, and where you feel it's deserving. Ten to 20 percent, with 15 percent being the norm.

Money Changers

Banks and hotels, with hotels offering a lower exchange rate. Bank of Hawaii and First Hawaiian Bank have the most branches statewide. Street changers are nonexistent.

GETTING AROUND

Taxis

Airports and in Waikiki, not so common elsewhere on Oahu and the neighboring islands. Don't expect to flag down one on the street. If a taxi is required, go to a nearby hotel. Or use the telephone to summon one. Rates are metered, although for long trips, a flat rate may be negotiated. Aloha State Cab, tel: 847 3566. Charley's Taxi, tel: 531 1333. Sida Taxi, tel: 836 0011.

Right: only in Hawaii

Bus

Only Oahu has a comprehensive bus system, TheBus, and it is superb. Connections and frequency are excellent, and TheBus goes everywhere, including around the island. It is also affordable; flat fare one-way anywhere is US$1. For route or connection information, tel: 848 5555.

Car

The only practical transportation in most of Hawaii. Rates are among the cheapest in the world; competition is stiff, but be safe and book in advance. Weekly rates and air/hotel package rates are cheapest when booked in advance. Day rates with unlimited miles are standard. Hawaiian and Aloha Airlines offer good deals on neighboring islands, sometimes even on an hour's notice off-season. All the major car rental firms are represented. Credit card required, and an international driver's license often requested.

Right turns on red lights, after stopping, are okay.

Ferry

The only scheduled inter-island boat runs are offered by Trilogy Expeditions, linking Lahaina, Maui, with Manele Harbor on Lanai.

Inter-Island Flights

By commercial airlines, mostly by jet. Schedules are frequent and convenient, hourly on popular routes.

Flights average only ½ hour in the air. But add time on both ends for rental car pick up

and return, hotel check in and check out, ground travel time, and all those unexpected things that slow you down when rushed. I recommend budgeting 4 hours of total time.

The two main carriers are Aloha Airlines (and its subsidiary, IslandAir), and Hawaiian Airlines. For reservations call:

Aloha Airlines
Oahu, tel: 484 1111
Other islands, tel: (800) 367 5250
Hawaiian Airlines
Oahu, tel: 838 1555
Other islands, tel: (800) 367 5320

Disabled

Hawaii's visitor facilities are very good for those requiring special assistance. Most hotels offer facilities, including rooms, for those in wheelchairs. Request the *Aloha Guide for Persons with Disabilities* from the Commission on Persons with Disabilities, at 500 Ala Moana Boulevard, Suite 210, Honolulu 96813. Tel: (808) 586 8121. Hawaii Visitors Bureau has a guide called *Aloha Guide to Accessibility*.

ACCOMMODATION

Hotels

There is a wide range of accommodations to suit all pockets and tastes. As with everywhere, the quality of the hotel is commensurate with price. Published rates for a double room (excluding the 9.25 percent room tax) are categorized as follows: $ = under US$100, $$ = US$100–150, $$$ = over US$150. Make sure to ask for bargains,

discounts, special room and car packages, and off-season deals from travel agents and airlines or the hotels directly.

Oahu

Halekulani Hotel
2199 Kalia Road, Honolulu 96815
Waikiki
Tel: 923 2311 Fax: 922 5111
Toll: (800) 367 2343
Nobody disagrees: Waikiki's finest hotel. Mood and atmosphere seem independent of the Waikiki bustle despite prime location. Sophisticatedly discreet decor and staff. *$$$*

Ihilani Resort & Spa
1001 Olani St, Kapolei 96707
West Oahu
Tel: 679 0079 Fax: 679 0080
Toll: (800) 626 4446
Blazing trails to west Oahu, this luxury resort has a neighboring island feel, glitzy multi-level spa, and a picture-perfect swimming cove. *$$$*

Kahala Mandarin Oriental
5000 Kahala Avenue, Honolulu 96816
Tel: 734 2211 Fax: 737 2478
Toll: (800) 367 2525
Away from everything, but then not. Popular with statesmen and celebrities, it is casually exquisite and elegantly affluent. After a night, it feels like home. *$$$*

Royal Hawaiian Hotel
2259 Kalakaua Avenue, Honolulu 96815
Tel: 923 7311 Fax: 924 7098
Toll: (800) 782 9488

Opened in 1927, the Royal remains the quintessential Waikiki hotel. Rooms have been upgraded and public areas still have period-piece charm. It faces prime beach-front and, for Waikiki, has extensive grounds. *$$$*

Manoa Valley Inn
2001 Vancouver Drive, Honolulu 96822
Manoa Valley
Tel: 947 6019 Fax: 946 6168
Toll: (800) 634 5115
Formerly the John Guild Inn, a 1920s mansion of 7 bedrooms. Above Waikiki in Manoa Valley, where it's quiet, cool, and a little more wet. *$$*

New Otani Kaimana Beach Hotel
2863 Kalakaua Avenue, Honolulu 96815
Edge of Waikiki
Tel: 923 1555 Fax: 922 9404
Toll: (800) 356 8264
Near Diamond Head and Kapiolani Park, away from central Waikiki. Known as a pleasant alternative to more expensive Waikiki hotels. Rooms are sometimes quite small, but nice. *$$*

Turtle Bay Hilton and Country Club
57–091 Kamehameha Highway,
Kahuku 96731, North Shore
Tel: 293 8811 Fax: 293 9147
Toll: (800) HILTONS
Far from anywhere, with rugged views of the North Shore. A good retreat choice, whether for golf or for staring at the horizon. *$$*

Waikiki Joy Hotel
320 Lewers Street, Honolulu 96815
Tel: 923 2300 Fax: 924 4010
Toll: (800) 422 0450
Despite its name, popular for its upscale atmosphere and boutique size. Away from the beach and scenery, but pleasant. Out of the ordinary. *$$*

Waikiki Parc
2233 Helumoa Road, Honolulu 96815
Tel: 921 7272 Fax: 923 1336

Toll: (800) 422 0450
An affordable alternative to the Halekulani (same management). Back from the beach. An economical class act with the Halekulani's grace. Stunning ocean views higher up. *$$*

Big Island
Four Seasons Resort Hualalai
P O Box 1269, Kailua-Kona 96745
North Kona
Tel: 325 8000 Fax: 325 8100
Toll: (888) 340 3442
Bali-style elegance defines this hotel, which offers uncrowded golf, three large swimming pools, full service spa, beautifully landscaped grounds, great dining options and the best cultural facility of any hotel in the islands. *$$$*

Kona Village Resort
P O Box 1299, Kailua-Kona 96745
North Kona
Tel: 325 5555 Fax: 325 5124
Toll: (800) 367 5290
Nothing else like it in Hawaii. Individual luxury *hales* with no telephones or TVs. No coats or ties permitted. Lose track of time and reality here. *$$$*

Mauna Kea Beach Hotel
One Mauna Kea Beach Drive,
Kohala Coast 96743
Tel: 882 7222 Fax: 882 7552
Toll: (800) 882 6060
The original Big Island luxury resort, newly-renovated but still possessing its original charm, a beautiful beach, and museum-quality Asian and Pacific art throughout. *$$$*

Mauna Lani Bay Hotel & Bungalows
1 Mauna Lani Drive,
Kohala Coast 96743
Tel: 885 6622 Fax: 885 4556
Toll: (800) 367 2323
Kohala's best, with less theatrics than its neighbors, and peerless service, ambiance, and style. Ancient fishponds, petroglyph fields, and other historical spots nearby. *$$$*

Opposite: the landmark Royal Hawaiian Hotel

Hawaii Naniloa Hotel
93 Banyan Drive, Hilo 96720
Tel: 969 3333 Fax: 969 6622
Toll: (800) 367 5360
This recently-refurbished and pleasant hotel on Banyan Drive is unquestionably Hilo's best choice. Great views of bay and Mauna Kea volcano. *$$*

Holualoa Inn
P O Box 222, Holualoa 96725, Near Kona
Tel: 324 1121 Fax: 324 1121
Perched in a small artists' town above Kona, this is a very quiet place of quality. Better than any typical bed-and-breakfast place. A fireplace, even. *$$*

Kilauea Lodge
P O Box 116, Volcano 96785
Tel: 967 7366 Fax: 967 7367
An estate built in the 1930s, it offers 11 rooms, several with fireplaces. Cool and quiet, with a classy restaurant. *$$*

Royal Kona Resort
75–5852 Alii Drive, Kailua-Kona 96740
Tel: 329 3111 Fax: 329 9532
Toll: (800) 774 5662
Excellent location near downtown Kona, on the harbor. Sometimes busy, but with wonderful views and ambiance. *$$*

The Royal Waikoloan
69–275 Waikoloa Beach Drive,
Waikoloa 96743

Tel: 885 6789 Fax: 885 7852
Toll: (800) 688 7444
It's impossible to be disappointed with this graceful and unpretentious hotel, with a beautiful oceanfront and ancient Hawaiian fishponds. A 20-minute drive from Keahole Kona Airport. *$$*

Manago Hotel
P O Box 145, Capt Cook 96704
South Kona
Tel: 323 2642
An island classic, far from everything noisy and shiny. A friendly family-run place with a down-home restaurant and even a Japanese-style room. *$*

Kauai
Hyatt Regency Kauai
1571 Poipu Road, Koloa 96756
Tel: 742 1234 Fax: 742 1577
Toll: (800) 233 1234
The best and nicest in Poipu. Open-air courtyards, low-rise architecture and subdued elegance. Right on the beach. *$$$*

Kauai Marriott Resort & Beach Club
Kalapaki Beach, Lihue 96766
Tel: 245 5050 Fax: 245 5049
Toll: (800) 228 9290
Formerly the Westin but less ostentatious than its predecessor. Horse-drawn carriages, lagoon boat tours, and Kauai's biggest swimming pool. Check out the weekly Comedy Club for some laughs. *$$$*

Princeville Hotel
P O Box 3069, Princeville 96722
North Shore
Tel: 826 9644 Fax: 826 1166
Toll: (800) 782 9488
Recently renovated, a no-holds-barred hotel of luxury with Hawaii's finest view. Indulge in both. One of Hawaii's friendliest hotel staffs. The soft smell of flowers everywhere. *$$$*

Hanalei Bay Resort
P O Box 220, Hanalei 96714
Tel: 826 6522 Fax: 826 6680
Tol: (800) 827 4427
Perched on a cliff, it offers the same north shore views as its neighbor, the Princeville Hotel, but at slightly lower prices. Units have kitchens. *$$*

Hanalei Colony Resort
P O Box 206, Hanalei 96714
North Shore
Tel: 826 6235 Fax: 826 9893
Toll: (800) 628 3004
Better for families than recluses, comfortable but simple (no TVs) condo units are right on the beach. Last hotel on the road heading north. *$$*

Koke`e Lodge
P O Box 819 Waimea 96796
Koke`e/Waimea Canyon
Tel: 335 6061
A dozen simple but fully-equipped cabins in Koke`e State Park. Nothing but what's necessary. Popular and often booked. *$*

Mauai
Four Seasons Resort
3900 Wailea Alanui, Wailea 96753
Tel: 874 8000 Fax: 874 2222
Toll: (800) 334 MAUI
Ocean views and attention to details everywhere. Princely luxury but so subdued, it never feels crowded or busy. *$$$*

Hotel Hana-Maui
P O Box 8, Hana 96713
Tel: 248 8211 Fax: 248 7202
Toll: (800) 321 HANA

The epitome of an exclusive hiding place (97 rooms), with large doses of luxurious Hawaiian atmosphere. And then there's the Hana Coast all around. *$$$*

Kapalua Bay Hotel & Villas
1 Bay Drive, Lahaina 96761, West Maui
Tel: 669 5656 Fax: 669 4694
Toll: (800) 367 8000
Smooth and embracing, a Mediterranean-style place for hiding or golf and lots of tranquility. *$$$*

Kapalua Villas
500 Office Road, Kapalua 96761
Tel: 669 8088 Fax: 669 5234
Toll: (800) 545 0018
Nicely situated selection of spacious condominium with shuttle links to the rest of the resort. *$$$*

Kea Lani Hotel, Suites & Villas
4100 Wailea Alanui, Wailea 96753
Tel: 875 4100 Fax: 875 1200
Toll: (800) 659 4100
Beautifully landscaped grounds, a great beach, plus spacious suites make this Wailea property a good choice. *$$$*

Renaissance Wailea Beach Resort
3550 Wailea Alanui Drive, Wailea 96753
Tel: 879 4900 Fax: 874 5370
Toll: (800) 992 4532
Consistently recognized for over a decade as one of the best. Lush, luxurious, personal but comprehensive. Romantic quiet beach. *$$$*

Westin Maui
2365 Ka`anapali Parkway, Lahaina 96761
West Maui
Tel: 667 2525 Fax: 661 5831
Toll: (800) 228 3000
Twelve acres of water, and more water. The Westin has set the Ka`anapali standard for elegance. Punctuated with Asian and Pacific art. *$$$*

Maui Marriott
100 Nohea Kai Drive, Lahaina 96761

practical information

West Maui
Tel: 667 1200 Fax: 661 8575
Toll: (800) 228 9290
Modest amidst the sparkle of nearby 'fantasy' resorts. Most rooms have ocean views. Comfortable, tasteful, and unpretentious. Friendly, relaxed staff. *$$–$$$*

Lahaina Hotel
127 Lahainaluna Road, Lahaina 96761
Tel: 661 0577 Fax: 667 9480
Toll: (800) 669 3444
Built in the 1860s, wonderfully restored with beautiful antiques and attention to detail. Near the waterfront. Romantic with cozy luxury. *$$*

Silver Cloud Ranch
RR II, Box 201, Kula 96790
Tel: 878 6101 Fax: 878 2132
Toll: (800) 532 1111
A great upcountry alternative to the beachfront scene, with charming rooms, communal breakfast, and panoramic views of the coast from a setting 4,000ft up on the slopes of Haleakala. *$$*

The Plantation Inn
174 Lahainaluna Road, Lahaina 96761
Tel: 667 9225 Fax: 667 9293
Toll: (800) 433 6815
A new place but with plantation ambiance and details. A romantic and quiet alternative to the resorts, but with a modest swimming pool. *$$*

Molokai
The Camps at Molokai Ranch
P O Box 259, Maunaloa 96770, Molokai
Tel: 552 2791 Fax: 552 2330
Toll: (800) 254 8871
Three upscale wilderness campsites with all you'll need to feel pampered. Tranquility, privacy, plenty of aloha, and a range of activities that add up to a unique experience. *$$$*

Kaluakoi Hotel & Golf Club
P O Box 1977, Maunaloa 96770, Molokai
Tel: 552 2555 Fax: 552 2821

Toll: (888) 552 2550
Nestled on Molokai's west end, you get comfort and quiet in concert with the beautiful Kepuhi Beach. *$$*

Lanai
Manele Bay Hotel/Lodge at Koele
P O Box 774, Lanai City 96763, Lanai
Tel: 565 7700 Fax: 565 6744
Toll: (800) 321 4666
Lush, sensuous, Manele Bay is the tropical beach counterpart to the **Lodge at Koele** (same address, but located higher up in the hills). *$$$*

Bed & Breakfast

Hawaii's Best Bed & Breakfast
P O Box 563, Kamuela 96743
Tel: 885 4550 Fax: 885 0559
Toll: (800) 262 9912

Pacific Hawaii Bed & Breakfast
1312 Aulepe Street, Kailua 96734
Tel: 486 8838 Fax: 261 6573
Toll: (800) 999 6026

Bed & Breakfast Hawaii
P O Box 449, Kapa`a 96746
Tel: 822 7771 Fax: 822 2723
Toll: (800) 733 1632
Condominiums.

Aston Hotels and Resorts
2155 Kalakaua Avenue, Suite 500,
Honolulu 96815
Tel: 923 0745 Fax: 922 8785
Toll: (800) 922 7866
Call for information on its properties on the major Hawaiian islands. Most offer good value for money.

HOURS & HOLIDAYS

Business Hours
Hawaii wakes up early, and most people are in their offices by 8am. Office hours are typically 8am to 5pm, Monday through Friday. Shopping centers open between 9.30am and

10am, closing around 9pm. Banks are open 8.30am to 3pm, Monday to Thursday; until 6pm on Fridays.

Public Holidays

All US national holidays, plus two additional state holidays: Prince Kuhio Day on March 26, and Kamehameha Day on June 11.

USEFUL ADDRESSES

Hawaii Visitors & Convention Bureau (HVCB)

Hawaii

Oahu, Waikiki: *Business Plaza, 8th Floor, Honolulu 96815*
Tel: 923 1811
In the middle of Waikiki and with tons of information for the taking.
Big Island, Hilo: Tel: 961 5797
Big Island, Kailua-Kona: Tel: 329 7787
Kauai, Lihue: Tel: 245 3971
Maui, Kahului: Tel: 244 3530

North America

Canada
1260 Hornby Street, Suite 104
Vancouver, B C V6Z 1W2
Tel: (604) 669 6691
San Francisco
180 Montgomery Street, #2360
San Francisco, CA 94104
Tel: (415) 248 3800

International

United Kingdom
P O Box 208, Sunbury on Thames
Middx TW16 5RJ
Tel: (44) 181 941 4009
Fax: (44) 181 941 4011
Germany
Siemensstrasse 9, 63263 Neu-Isenburg
Tel: (49) 61 02 72 2411
Fax: (49) 61 02 72 2409
South America
Dr Mario Cassinoni, 1676 OF 308
11200 Montevideo, Uruguay
Tel: (598) 2 402 4171
Fax: (598) 2 402 5493

MUSEUMS

Oahu

Bishop Museum
1525 Bernice Street, Honolulu 96817
Tel: 847 3511
Daily 9am to 5pm. Planetarium daily 11am, 2pm, and Friday, Saturday 7pm.

Children's Discovery Center
111 Ohe Street, Kakaako, Honolulu
Tel: 522 8910
Hands-on exhibits and play station with discovery as the theme.

Contemporary Museum of Art
2411 Makiki Heights Drive, Honolulu
Tel: 526 0232
Daily, 10am to 4pm; Sunday, noon to 4pm.

Hawaii's Plantation Village
94–695 Waipahu Street, Waipahu
Tel: 677 0110
A hybrid plantation village comprised of homes representing each of the ethnic groups who came to islands to work the canefields.

Honolulu Academy of Arts
900 S Beretania Street, Honolulu
Tel: 538 1006
Tuesday to Saturday, 10am to 4.30pm; Sunday, 1pm to 5pm.

HAWAII VISITORS BUREAU MARKER

Kauai

Grove Farm Homestead Museum
Nawiliwili Road, on the outskirts of Lihue
Tel: 245 3202
Open Monday, Wednesday and Thursday for 2-hour long tours of an authentically preserved plantation manager's home, portions of which date to the mid-19th century.

Kauai Museum
4428 Rice Street, Lihue 96766
Tel: 245 6931
Open Monday to Friday, 9am to 4.30pm; Saturday, 9am to 1pm.

Waiole Mission House
Tel: 245 3202
It is in Hanalei, yet hidden behind the grassy acres that surround the Hanalei Mission, the Mission Home, Waiole is a survivor from the 1830s, a classic look back in time. Open Monday to Friday, 10am to 3pm.

Maui

Bailey House Museum/Hale Ho`ike`ike
Home to the Maui Historical Society, Wailuku
Tel: 244 3326
This missionary homestead dates back to the 1830s. Interesting Mauiana on display.

Baldwin Home Museum
120 Dickenson Street, Lahaina
Tel: 661 3262

The beautifully restored home of medical Missionary Dwight Baldwi.

Whalers Village Museum/Hale Kohala
Whalers Village Shopping Complex, Lahaina 96761
Tel: 661 5992
Located in the Ka`anapali resort area. Open daily, 9.30am to 10pm.

HEALTH & EMERGENCIES

Hygiene / General Health
The same standards as Europe and North America. Hawaii offers world-class medical care. Note that the United States doesn't have a national health plan; most hospital care is paid by private insurance or health plans. Tap water everywhere is safe. Don't drink stream or river water.

Crime / Trouble
Hawaii is one of the safest places in the United States. Still, take the usual precautions as anywhere else. There can be problems at beach and lookout parking lots: rental cars stand out like intergalactic supernovas. Lock cars and don't leave valuables inside.

Police
Honest, professional and reliable. Can't be talked out of speeding tickets. Most officers use their own cars on neighbor islands and on Oahu outside of Waikiki. In other words, most police cars are unmarked and don't look like government-issued police cars, save for a very small single blue light on the roof. The radar is widely used.

COMMUNICATIONS & NEWS

Post
Domestic US rates apply within Hawaii and to the mainland; it costs the same to mail a letter within Honolulu as to New York. Domestic and international express mail service is available, as are most international courier

Left: happy Hawaiian family

services, including Federal Express, DHL and United Parcel. Customer information, tel: (800) 275 8777. Most hotels also provide postal services.

Telephone

Area code for all islands is 808. Toll-free calls: dial 800 or 888, then the number. Inter-island calls are toll calls: dial 1-808 before the seven-digit number. To call abroad directly, first dial the international access code 011, followed by the country code: Australia (61); France (33); Germany (49); Japan (81); Netherlands (31); Spain (34); UK (44); US and Canada (1). If using a US credit phone card, dial the company's access number, followed by 01, then the country code. Sprint, tel: 10 333. AT&T, tel: 10 288.

Media

All major American broadcast and cable television networks are available. Several local stations broadcast programs in Japanese, Korean and other Asian languages. There are two statewide daily newspapers – the morning *Advertiser* and the afternoon *Star-Bulletin*. Neighboring islands have their own daily newspapers. Mainland newspapers are widely available at bookstores and large supermarkets.

USEFUL INFORMATION

Children

Children are welcome everywhere. Many of the larger hotels offer special programs and activities for children. Remember, however, that some high-end hotels are known for quiet and privacy, and noisy children may vanish without a trace.

Maps

Available almost everywhere, especially bookstores. Best are the University of Hawaii Press maps, by James Bier (white cover with blue-and-green letters) and the Insight Pocket Map which comes with this guide. Also, all rental car companies offer free booklets with simple road maps

LANGUAGE

English and Hawaiian are the official languages. English is the language of commerce, business, education, and nearly everything else. The exception is Ni`ihau, where Hawaiian is spoken. Also spoken are Japanese, Chinese, Korean, Samoan, Vietnamese, and the local patois, called pidgin English.

FURTHER READING

Atlas of Hawaii, by University of Hawaii. The best reference book for information and maps covering nearly every aspect of Hawaii: geology, environment, social and economic structure.

Hawaii's Birds, by the Hawaii Audubon Society. Birdwatchers need this, as do those wondering what that pesky bird with the red head and gray body is.

Hawaiian Mythology, by Martha Beckwith. The unquestioned standard for decades. Good for a month of reading.

The Art of the Hula, by Allan Seiden. An excellent, beautifully illustrated introduction to Hawaii's national dance.

Mark Twain's Letters from Hawaii, by Mark Twain. Reprinted letters from when Twain was a newspaper correspondent.

Place Names of Hawaii, by Mary K Pukui and others. This is the best guide to the meaning of Hawaiian place names.

Shoal of Time: A History of the Hawaiian Islands, by Gavan Daws. A superb book of Hawaii's history after Western contact, from Cook's arrival to the 1960s.

Stories of Hawaii, by Jack London. Paperback reprint of this famous writer, who traveled in Hawaii in 1907.

Volcanoes in the Sea: The Geology of Hawaii, by Gordon A MacDonald and others. The definitive book on the geological history of the Hawaiian islands.

Waikiki Beachboy, by Grady Timmons. A hardcover book covering the history and lifestyle of the beachboy.

Insight Guide: Hawaii, by Apa Publications, Singapore. Captures the exquisite beauty of the islands with insightful features and stunning photography.

Also from Insight Guides...

Insight Guides is the classic series, providing the complete picture with expert and informative text and stunning photography. Each book is an ideal travel planner, a reliable on-the-spot companion – and a superb visual souvenir of a trip. 193 titles.

Insight Maps are designed to complement the guidebooks. They provide full mapping of major destinations, and their laminated finish gives them ease of use and durability. 65 titles.

Insight Compact Guides are handy reference books, modestly priced yet comprehensive. The text, pictures and maps are all cross-referenced, making them ideal books to consult while seeing the sights. 119 titles.

INSIGHT POCKET GUIDE TITLES

Aegean Islands	California,	Israel	Moscow	Seville, Cordoba &
Algarve	Northern	Istanbul	Munich	Granada
Alsace	Canton	Jakarta	Nepal	Seychelles
Amsterdam	Chiang Mai	Jamaica	New Delhi	Sicily
Athens	Chicago	Kathmandu Bikes	New Orleans	Sikkim
Atlanta	Corsica	& Hikes	New York City	Singapore
Bahamas	Costa Blanca	Kenya	New Zealand	Southeast England
Baja Peninsula	Costa Brava	Kuala Lumpur	Oslo and	Southern Spain
Bali	Costa Rica	Lisbon	Bergen	Sri Lanka
Bali Bird Walks	Crete	Loire Valley	Paris	Sydney
Bangkok	Denmark	London	Penang	Tenerife
Barbados	Fiji Islands	Los Angeles	Perth	Thailand
Barcelona	Florence	Macau	Phuket	Tibet
Bavaria	Florida	Madrid	Prague	Toronto
Beijing	Florida Keys	Malacca	Provence	Tunisia
Berlin	French Riviera	Maldives	Puerto Rico	Turkish Coast
Bermuda	(Côte d'Azur)	Mallorca	Quebec	Tuscany
Bhutan	Gran Canaria	Malta	Rhodes	Venice
Boston	Hawaii	Manila	Rome	Vienna
Brisbane & the	Hong Kong	Marbella	Sabah	Vietnam
Gold Coast	Hungary	Melbourne	St. Petersburg	Yogjakarta
British Columbia	Ibiza	Mexico City	San Francisco	Yucatán Peninsula
Brittany	Ireland	Miami	Sarawak	
Brussels	Ireland's	Montreal	Sardinia	
Budapest	Southwest	Morocco	Scotland	

ACKNOWLEDGEMENTS

10	**Jacques Arago**
42	**Ron Dahlquist**
70	**Catherine Karnow**
1, 5B, 6B, 7B, 16, 20, 21, 23, 26, 27(top & bottom), 28(top & bottom), 30(top & bottom), 31, 32(bottom), 33(top & bottom), 46, 47, 48(bottom), 53(top), 54(top & bottom), 55, 56(top & bottom), 64, 67(top & bottom), 68, 69, 71, 73, 74, 78, 80, 82, 83, 84, 88, 89, 91, 92, 94, 96, 97, 98	**Mark Read**
15	**Robert Van Dyke Collection**
2/3, 4, 5(top), 6(top), 8/9, 12(top & bottom), 24, 25, 29, 34, 35, 36, 40, 41, 43, 44(top & bottom), 48(top), 49, 52, 53(bottom), 57, 58, 59, 61, 62, 63, 65, 66, 72, 75, 77, 79, 86, 90	**Scott Rutherford**
7(top), 11	**Marc Schechter/Photo Resource Hawaii**
13	**Terence Barrow Collection**
Cartography	**Berndston & Berndston**

INDEX